Kama Sutra

Master the Art of Sex through Ancient Teachings and Love Making Techniques

Veronica Baruwal

Disclaimer Notice:

Table of Contents

Veronica Baruwal

Introduction

The Kama Sutra and the knowledge contained within it have changed lives in such a significant way that those who have read it want to share that knowledge with as many people as possible. This desire to spread knowledge is the primary reason behind this book!

Within this document you are going to find in depth information regarding what exactly Kama Sutra is. The ancient teachings of sex and love have much to teach us, especially in a day and age where we have become increasingly disconnected from one another. They are extremely important and can be very beneficial in a lot of ways.

The main thing you need to recognize if you are to gain anything from this book is that Kama Sutra is not just about having mind-blowing sex. It's a total mindset, and a way of life to which both partners should be committed if they are to reap all the benefits – physical, emotional, and sexual - that the Kama Sutra has to offer. It may be ancient teaching, but it is still entirely relevant today, around 1700 years after it was compiled. There are lessons to be taken away from this, but you need to be receptive to them, since some of the practices may seem strange – particularly to Western sensibilities.

With all of the relevant information at hand, you can begin practicing Kama Sutra without worrying about going through a dense book. Apply the ancient sexual knowledge of Hinduism and improve your love life and sex life immensely!

Chapter 1
What is Kama Sutra?

As a society, human beings have evolved to a point where many of the issues that we once faced are no longer valid. Things like hunger and the threat of violence are no longer factors that we need to consider as we get on with our lives.

However, as people have become progressively safer and more comfortable, they have formed a tendency to retreat into themselves. With so much technology to give them the illusion of human contact, they have stopped truly connecting with other human beings, and for a lot of people this has begun to affect their sex lives, and even their everyday lives.

This is probably why so much research is now being conducted into alternative sexual practices. These practices are not so much fetishes, as ideologies that can demonstrate how people can love each other better, and with this better love naturally follows better sex and increased intimacy.

It seems today that the majority of sexual practices and ideologies that are particularly effective are based on ancient texts created by societies that were more in tune with their inner selves, and thus able to provide insight that is extremely useful. They saw sex as something sacred to be enjoyed, rather than something sinful to be avoided, and they were eager to share their viewpoints with others so that they too might be more sexually fulfilled.

There is no society in the world that is older than Indian society, which means that these ancient people probably have access to secrets of the deepest and most private aspects of human sexuality. A Hindu text on sexuality is a formidable thing to think about, as it would probably have a lot of very potent information contained within.

The ancient Hindu text that is being discussed here is the Kama Sutra, and it is perhaps the oldest book in the world that was dedicated to love, insights into successful relationships, and ultimately, through the review and perfection of these things, the improvement of one's sex life.

However, the Kama Sutra is unique in other aspects as well. Not only is this book the first of its kind, it is the only ancient text about sex that provides detailed instructions on how to become a better lover, along with diagrams for positions that, when used, can provide unimaginable pleasure during sex.

The Kama Sutra is such a detailed document that reading it even in the modern day and age that we currently live in can provide us with incredible enlightenment regarding sex. We can potentially learn things that we would never even have thought of about sex and the art of lovemaking!

The Kama sutra is said to have been compiled in the 200 BC by Vatsyayana, who was a saint or a monk based in northern India.

He is said to have been inspired to come up with the book in a bid to grow close to god. The authenticity of this story has been questioned by many scholars as Vatsyayana is said to have been a celibate monk who sought to grow closer to the deity by coming up with the different illustrations.

However, Vatsyayana is only credited for having assembled the book; the ideologies all belonged to different people. Many believe that several artists and authors at the time had come up with poems and illustrations, which Vatsyayana compiled into a book.

The book has now been translated into various languages and is said to be a universal book on the topic of love, sex, and relationships.

The word Kama sutra translates to "treatise of pleasure" and is meant to be a textbook of sorts for people to refer and enhance their sexual experience.

Kama deva is said to have been the love of god. He is generally depicted as having green skin and carries with him a bow made out of sugar cane. He launches a set of arrows that are made from aligned bees and makes two people fall in love with each other.

There was a time when a demon named Tarakasur was troubling Earthlings. Indira, the god of lightening, came to know that an offspring of lord Shiva could defeat Tarakasur and restore peace on earth.

But Lord Shiva was without child and so, Indira decided to take the help of Kama to get lord Shiva to fall in love with goddess Parvathi.

Kama is said to have disturbed Shiva during his meditation, which caused him to burn Kama down to the ground. Kama's wife is said to have begged and pleaded for her husband to be resurrected and Shiva obeyed her and brought Kama to life.

Since then, Kama is worshipped as the god of love and people wanting to find their ideal partner pay obeisance to him.

He is often compared to cupid - the god of love according to Greek mythology. His antics are generally thought to be the basis for the Kama sutra.

Back in the day, women were forced to get married and parents of girls would look for an ideal groom based on their status. The girls would not be interested in their grooms and thereby not enjoy sex fully. In order to solve the issue, the Kama sutra was used to help women enjoy their sexual experiences. It taught men to love and embrace their ladies and allow them to have a pleasurable experience.

A second book was then released a while later known as the Kamashastra and is said to have further exploited the topic. We will look at it in detail in a later chapter of this book.

The basic tenet however is to increase the sexual pleasure with your partner. This point is reiterated as it involves around the basic principle of the males finding their ideal mate and pleasuring her to give them the best offspring.

The Kama sutra lays down a lot of emphasis on the importance of married couples exploiting their true sexual nature and growing close to each other. This is especially pertinent in today's age where everybody is busy and not really interested in nurturing relationships.

What the Kama Sutra can truly contribute to modern society lies in its deepest secrets. Within the Kama Sutra lie sex positions that would have taken a true sexual genius to think of. These sex positions are so intensely erotic that just the act of getting into them can provide more stimulation than you might have felt through actual regular sex!

The modern perception of Kama Sutra tends to focus on this aspect of what Kama Sutra is. However, this ancient text has a lot more to offer than simply new sex positions, although these sex positions do form a significant part of the knowledge that this book can impart.

The Kama Sutra provides an ideology that you can apply in order to be better at sex. This is more than sex positions; it involves detailed and specific tips regarding what to do during sex, and information about how you can better seduce a woman. It also involves living a lifestyle dedicated to virtuous and prosperous living, and freely enjoying life's sensual and sensory pleasures.

By applying the rules and principles of Kama Sutra, you can become a phenomenal lover, but in order to do this you must first familiarize yourself with the basic rules of Kama Sutra, which will be briefly explained in the next chapter.

Veronica Baruwal

Chapter 2
What the Kama Sutra Says About Sex

The most important aspect of Kama Sutra is not the sex positions, but what it dictates is proper during sex. By applying the rules and lessons provided in this chapter you can be better at sex, it is true, but you can also become a better lover overall. The thing to remember is that, according to the Kama Sutra, sex is not sinful, but bad sex is something to be avoided. The word Kama means pleasure, and that should give you the clue about what this ancient text is trying to achieve.

By having sex the Kama Sutra way, you can truly make your partner feel loved, and provide a sexual experience that would awaken the very essence of their soul. By applying these lessons, you can make sex a spiritual experience!

A Woman Must Be Knowledgeable about Sex

People generally think of the past as a horrible place for women. This is because women did not have rights and were forced into marriages that they wanted no part of. Women were not supposed to have anything to do with sex, despite the fact that they were considered to be good for just that one thing. The main assumption was that if a woman actually enjoyed sex, she was a wicked woman, and not the type a man wanted to choose for a wife.

It is natural to assume such a thing, but if you were to read Kama Sutra, you would discover that ancient Indian society had a different take on the matter.

According to the Kama Sutra, a woman must be as knowledgeable about sex as possible. This means that you, as a woman, must know as many sex positions as possible. You must be willing to learn in bed as well, willing to discover your own body.

One of the things that Kama Sutra recommends the most is masturbation. This is because masturbation is the best way for a woman to discover her own body! If she is aware of her own body and how to derive pleasure from it, she will be able to take command during sex and make her man pleasure her in the ways she wants.

Size Matters

It does, but not in the way you think. Certain sizes are just more compatible with certain vaginas. A large penis, for example, is not quite compatible with a very tight vagina as there will be too much pain for pleasure to occur.

One tip that Kama Sutra provides is that smaller penises can be more useful. This is because they allow the woman more room to squeeze her thighs together and perform kegels during sex for maximum pleasure. Hence, size does matter. The smaller the better! There is also advice on positioning the legs to facilitate easy entry, even for large penises.

Live a Healthy Lifestyle

The reason so many people are unable to have fulfilling and satisfying sex lives is because they are not living healthy lifestyles. Sex is an extremely physical process, which means that your physical health is going to play a very important role in determining how sex is going to feel to you.

If you have a terrible diet or you do not exercise regularly, you are most likely going to have a poor sex life. You have to exercise and build on your stamina. Trying to have sex without eating a proper meal will prevent you from satisfying your partner. If you want to improve in this area, try taking up yoga. Yoga is an ancient exercise practice that makes you get into certain positions and avail a proper work out. The positions are all aimed at helping you perform the different contortions. In fact, there are certain positions in the Kama sutra that might entirely by inspired by yoga. Practicing them might help you get into these positions with ease. It is also recommended that you avoid meat if you want to be truly good at sex!

Consent is Important

One extremely important fact that is stated within the book of Kama Sutra is that it is very important to be positive of consent before having sex.

Apart from the initial "yes," you need to ensure that consent remains throughout the act. This can be done by taking it slow. Seduce your woman; make it so that she has every opportunity to tell you what she wants.

Too much of sex these days has become just relentless thrusting with absolutely no foreplay. Foreplay is important not just to arouse your partner, but also to give her ample time to consent to what you are about to do! And of course, foreplay helps the vagina to self-lubricate, which means that intercourse is more comfortable for both partners, whatever the man's penis size.

Mix Up Your Sex Positions

One point that the Kama Sutra emphasizes quite emphatically is that it is important to keep things fresh during sex. As is the case with most things in life, if you keep doing the same thing over and over again, eventually you will become bored. And even if sex is an amazing experience that you and your partner can have, there is no guarantee that it will not get monotonous for you. If you keep it as simple and bland as always, you will surely get bored with it in no time at all. So, you have to introduce a little variety and spice up your sex life.

This is why so many sex positions have been described in the Kama Sutra. You are supposed to use every single one! Try to find sex positions that complement each other so that you don't have to wait too long while getting into the next position, as that might kill the mood.

Kissing is Key

One of the most important aspects of sex according to the Kama Sutra is kissing. It is highly recommended that you kiss every part of your partner's body during sex, as lips are the center of communication within your body, and using them to stimulate your partner conveys your sexual desire in the most potent way.

There are three basic types of kisses that you can apply. The first one is called the brushing kiss. This kiss is the same for both sexes. It essentially involves stroking your lips upon the area you want to kiss but not quite kissing it fully.

The brushing kiss can also involve hovering over your partner's body with your lips just barely touching the skin. Your partner's body will be anticipating a kiss, but will be constantly denied that pleasure. This will result in a mountain of sexual tension developing, with your partner eventually getting extremely aroused.

The second type of kiss is the measured kiss. This is your standard kiss that involves pressing your lips against whichever part of your partner's body you want to kiss. However, if you and your partner are kissing each other on the lips, the measured kiss tends to be different for each sex.

A woman giving a measured kiss will not take control of the kiss. She will place her lips upon her partner's but will not press against him. Instead, she will allow him to dictate where the kiss is going.

The final kiss is the throbbing kiss. This can be particularly effective when it is applied to a woman's "Yoni", her vagina.

The throbbing kiss involves extensive use of the tongue. For a woman, a throbbing kiss is receptive, which means that the man must penetrate your mouth with his tongue, and you can press your tongue against his.

These kisses are sure to set the right tone for the rest of the session. You have to remain a bit patient though and allow your partner to get into the right mood. These kisses need to be played out before the foreplay.

Sex Happens in Stages

If you are applying the principles of Kama Sutra, you are going to have to take it slow. According to the Kama Sutra, this is the proper way to have sex and once you start applying it you are going to discover that it is a lot more fun.

From courtship to seduction to foreplay to the act itself, Kama Sutra even describes how you can make your partner comfortable after sex has ended. These stages will be discussed in detail in a subsequent chapter.

Scratching is Recommended

A rather interesting fact about the Kama Sutra is that it recommends using your nails. Nails are the only sharp part of the human body, far sharper than teeth, which are far too blunt to provide adequate stimulation.

Using your teeth on your partner's back while he is on top of you is going to force him to unconsciously thrust deeper into you. This is going to cause you to clench your Yoni, something that will end up providing intense pleasure for both of you. You should consider using your nails on every part of your partner's body.

The Woman Must Achieve Orgasm before the Man

This is perhaps the most important rule of Kama Sutra sex. These days, sex has become somewhat lopsided. Men climax first and then provide satisfaction to the women.

However, this is not quite fair. Once a man climaxes, all desire for sex is now gone. This means that he will not be able to provide adequate satisfaction to his partner.

However, if a man has yet to climax, the pleasure he will provide will be intense because he will be desperate for his own orgasm as well.

In fact, Kama Sutra recommends that a man earn his orgasm by giving as many as possible to the woman.

Once the woman is fully satisfied, the man can climax. If you apply this rule, you will find that your orgasms will become more intense and more satisfying!

Sex is more than Just Penetration

The Kama Sutra is ancient. Thousands of years old, in fact. However, despite the fact that a book containing such important information was released so long ago, men still have the same misconceptions about sex.

One misconception that the Kama Sutra clears up is the one regarding penetration. During sex, women do not primarily derive pleasure through penetration. Their pleasure is instead derived from the stimulation of their clitoris and labia.

This is why oral sex is such an important part of Kama Sutra sex. By making your woman sufficiently stimulated, you will be able to make the actual penetration part of sex more enjoyable.

Kama Sutra sex also involves the stimulation of the G spot using a technique that will be described in a later chapter. Note that even internal stimulation will involve the fingers and not the penis, because the penis happens to be a rather inefficient tool for providing pleasure to women.

Veronica Baruwal

Chapter 3

The Stages of Sex

According to Kama Sutra, sex is a lot more than the act itself. In order to have good sex, you will need to make sure that the buildup to sex is adequate.

As a man, the responsibility for sex falls on your shoulders. The Kama Sutra posits that in order to attain the most pleasure for sex, a man must provide the most pleasure to his woman that he possibly can. This will, in turn, make his own pleasure from sex a lot more intense.

The First Stage: Courtship

Yes, according to the ancient knowledge present within the Kama Sutra, sex begins all the way from courtship. While you are courting a woman, you must provide her with what are essentially clues as to what your intentions are.

We tend to subconsciously apply the Kama Sutra rules for courtship, but a lot of us fail to realize how important it is to make a woman feel special before we attempt to seduce her.

Buy her flowers, make her happy, and when she is ready she will make it very clear to you. At this point you can move on to the second stage of sex.

The Second Stage: Seduction

While seducing a woman, it is very important to give her every opportunity to tell you that she is uncomfortable. This is because consent is a rather tricky thing and Kama Sutra realizes this.

Start with a gentle shoulder rub. Try to see if she is tense, and massage her as best you can in order to relax her. Be aware of her; try to see if something you are doing is making her uncomfortable.

Make sure the environment facilitates seduction. Light candles, dim the lights, and dress your best. Half of seduction is creating the ambiance.

The Third Stage: Foreplay

Once you have gotten her in the mood, foreplay plays an important role in getting her ready to climax. There are several tips provided within the Kama Sutra about foreplay that will be elaborated on in the next chapter.

The Fourth Stage: Sex

There are several sex positions that are talked about in the book of Kama Sutra. All of the most significant ones will be discussed in a later chapter.

Once you have gotten her aroused and ready for sex, make sure that you mix it up as much as you can. Apply as many techniques and use as many positions as possible to give her the sex of her life!

The Fifth Stage: Aftercare

Once both of you have climaxed, it is important to treat her right while she is exhausted too. Give her a massage; iron out any kinks that might remain even after she has achieved orgasm.

More importantly, talk to her! You two just shared something beautiful and profound. Talking about it will increase intimacy, and might even put you two in the mood for another round. If you apply the techniques provided in this book, you can be sure she'd be willing.

Chapter 4
Kama Sutra Foreplay

If you want a woman to enjoy sex with you, the best thing you can do is apply Kama Sutra foreplay techniques.

By giving her good foreplay, you can ensure that she is more receptive to you during sex. Stimulating her Yoni before the act of sex itself will make her more sensitive. As a result, it will probably end up taking you far less time to take her to orgasm.

Apply these techniques during the third stage of sex to get the best possible results.

Sweet Foods and Pleasant Smells

The Kama Sutra heavily recommends spoiling your partner before the two of you get into any actual sex. Feed your partner fruits or chocolates, anything that is sweet.

Sweetness is commonly associated with sensuality, and according to Kama Sutra if you feed your partner something sweet before the act of sex it is going to make him or her more sexually sensitive.

It is also important to note that the recommendation is to feed your partner with your own hand. It will not be nearly as effective if your partner simply eats something sweet on their own.

This is because the act of feeding someone something significantly boosts intimacy. It instills within them a sense of belonging, a sense of possessiveness, and this is an extremely important part of foreplay.

Additionally, you can make the room that the two of you are in smell as sweet as possible. Try not to use air fresheners, as the smell they provide is artificial and thus ineffectual. Instead, try to use flowers. If flowers are not available you can use scented candles, as they provide a comfortable ambiance to your room, thus improving the quality of the sexual encounter. You can also find and burn some natural incense sticks to set the right mood. There are many scents that are said to be great during sex as they act as mood enhancers. These include rose, jasmine, and sandal. A woman can also lure her partner by making use of vanilla. That is sure to get him into bed as soon as possible!

Some people also prefer to rub some sort of scent on themselves before the session. This further adds to the effectiveness of the experience. Say for example applying a little essential oil on the pulse points will help in spreading the pleasant smell and arousing your partner. However, you must try and use something that will not tamper with your natural scent. It should be mild yet effective.

Undressing and a Full Embrace

The act of undressing your partner is given extreme importance within Kama Sutra. Once again, your partner is not undressing him or herself for you, you are doing it for her.

This is another example of how Kama Sutra encourages oneness in all things. While you are undressing your partner you are going to feel a deep connection, so it is important to look him or her in the eyes while you are doing it. This will make the whole process seem a lot more sexual and intimate than if they were simply undressing themselves.

Once the both of you are undressed, you need to embrace. This does not mean that you simply hug; you need to actually get into your partner. You need to wrap your arms around each other and get as close as possible.

This will seem a bit awkward at first. We have become conditioned to not wanting people near us in our modern times, but during sex distance is the last thing you want. Press your body against the body of your partner and wrap your arms and legs around them. Squeeze your bodies together until there is no discernible border between the two of you.

Gentle Thrusting and Biting

If the two of you are sexually compatible, you will find that during the embrace you're Lingam, or penis, is already pressed against her Yoni, or vagina.

Hence, while the two of you are embracing you must start thrusting against her vagina as gently as possible. It is important that you stimulate her clitoris as you thrust, as this is going to provide her with intense sexual stimulation, thus arousing her greatly and making her much more receptive to the sex that you both are about to engage in.

Hence, the two of you will now be engaged in a gentle rocking motion. While you are thrusting, bite her gently on her neck. Proceed to bite her on other parts of her body as well. Essentially, any part you can kiss her is ripe for biting as well. Just make sure that you bite very, very gently.

You can bite her lips, breasts, nipples, and especially her clitoris. The clitoris is a very sensitive part of her Yoni, so bite it as gently as possible. When you do so, you will see the pleasure coursing through her body like electricity!

Allow Her to Dominate You

One of the most important aspects of Kama Sutra is that it does not dictate who is dominant during sex. If your partner wants to be more dominating, it is important that you allow her to do so.

Not allowing her to act out her sexual aggression will result in sexual frustration. There are times when women like to be dominated and when they want to dominate. You have to prepare for both and allow your woman to take charge. The more you constrain her, the more passionate that she gets. So you can delay it for a while but then allow her to dominate you. That will help the two of you have the most amazing experience and both of you will be left thoroughly satisfied by the experience.

However, if both of you are sexually dominant, the tension resulting from neither of you allowing the other to get on top can be extremely stimulating and will result in intense and passionate sex. It is recommended that both of you act on your sexual impulses.

Stimulate Using Your Nails

There are three different parts of the body that you must use your nails on during foreplay. The first for women is the back, and for men is the neck. By lightly scratching these parts of the body you can provide your partner with intense sexual stimulation.

The second part of the body is the same for both sexes: the chest. By using your nails on a woman's breasts you will make her a lot more sexually sensitive, which will in turn result in your thrusts providing her with a great deal more pleasure than they would have otherwise.

The third part of the body for men is their woman's hips, and for women are their man's buttocks. These parts of the body are very prone to sexual stimulation, but are often overlooked in modern sex.

If you are in the throes of passion, you can even use force while using your nails. This will probably leave a mark but the mark is going to be a sign of extreme sexual passion. The marks that nails can cause can serve as reminders of your sexual encounter whenever you are in need of recalling a pleasant memory.

Veronica Baruwal

Chapter 5
Kama Sutra Sex Positions

Now we are getting down to the most important information that Kama Sutra provides: sex positions!

Each of these sex positions provides a different benefit, and each of them can provide an enormous boost to your sex life. It is highly recommended that you try each of these sex positions out. Additionally, it is recommended that you try more than one of these sex positions in each of your sexual encounters.

Variety is the spice of life, and mixing it up will ensure that you and your partner enjoy yourselves to the maximum amount possible.

The Indrani

This is in many ways the quintessential Kama Sutra sex position. It is somewhat familiar but at the same time is just exotic enough to provide you with a boost in the bedroom.

In order to perform the Indrani, the woman must be lying on her back, and the man on his knees. The woman's lower back must then be placed upon his knees, with her legs up in the air.

The man can then penetrate the woman, spreading her legs and giving her as much support as possible. This position is quite advanced, so a basic level of physical fitness is recommended before attempting it.

The benefits of this position mostly revolve around the fact that it allows the man to penetrate the woman so deeply. Out of all of the positions that have been described in the Kama Sutra, few provide penetration as deep as the Indrani.

Apart from the erotic pleasure derived from extremely deep penetration, the Indrani also allows the man to stimulate the woman's G spot with his penis. This makes the Indrani one of the very few positions that can allow the man to give the woman an orgasm using just his penis.

The Toad

The missionary position is one that most people are well aware of. It is frequently said to be boring, and although this is not exactly true it is fair to say that if a little more excitement was added to the missionary position is wouldn't exactly be a bad thing.

The Toad is a way to make the missionary position a little more arousing. It essentially involves the woman lying on her back, but instead of her legs being spread open underneath the man; they are wrapped around his thighs.

The first major benefit that you will notice is that the penetration is a lot deeper than what you might get in the missionary position. This deeper penetration facilitates a more intimate sexual experience for both you and your partner.

Additionally, the partner who is being penetrated can use their legs wrapped around their partner's thighs to squeeze them. This squeezing can provide intense pleasure for both you and your partner.

You can also use your legs to coax your partner into thrusting faster or harder. This makes the Toad one of the few positions in which the woman is on her back and yet still dominant.

The Clasping Position

This position is quite intense, and it requires a bit of a stretch for both parties involved. In order to perform the clasping position, both of you will have to spread your legs away from each other and place one on top of the other.

When you do this, you are going to find it a lot easier to thrust. In fact, the thrusting is going to be almost perfect while you are in this position, and the penetration will be on par with positions such as the toad.

The main benefit that this position provides, however, has nothing to do with pleasure, although a great deal of pleasure is obviously involved.

What this position can really help you with is boosting the chances of conception. When the man climaxes, the ejaculate is going to be ejected in a way that very little will spill out, if any at all. Additionally, the position of the penis will ensure that the sperm will have the maximum chance of going through the cervix into the uterus.

This position is hence quite useful for couples that have been trying to get pregnant for a while but have not been very successful.

The Yawning Position

This position is a further boost to the missionary position. It is similar to the Toad but in many ways can be considered to be an even more advanced version of that position, providing the same intimacy and closeness as the missionary position with the added bonus of much deeper penetration.

In order to use this position, the woman will have to be on her back and the man on top of her, exactly the way the missionary position works. However, in the Yawning position, the woman will raise her legs and place them on her partner's shoulders.

This is a bit of a stretch but it will provide a much more intense sexual experience. This position provides a much deeper penetration than even the Toad can provide, but there are several fundamental differences between the sexual dynamic that this position facilitates and the one that is facilitated by using the Toad during sex.

During the Toad, the woman is on her back but she does have some degree of dominance over her man. This is because her legs are wrapped around his thighs, allowing her to coax him into thrusting harder or slowing down depending on what she wants.

However, the Yawning position puts the woman in a far more submissive position than even the missionary does. Since her legs are on his shoulders, she is afforded far less mobility than if her legs were spread out below her on the bed, which means that she will tend to feel more under his power than she would otherwise.

If you are aroused at the thought of being submissive to your partner, or if you are a man who wants a position in which he is dominant, the yawning position can be absolutely perfect for you.

The Nail Fixing Position

If you want to experience a more advanced version of the missionary position, one that is even more advanced than what the Toad can provide, but you do not want to be as submissive as you are during the Yawning position, you can use this position instead.

The Nail Fixing position is a very exotic looking position and it can place the man completely under your control. It is a firmly dominant sex position for the woman and can place the man completely within your power more completely than even the toad can.

This position essentially involves the woman lying on her back and stretching her legs back the same way they do in the Yawning position. However, instead of simply placing them on the man's shoulders, the woman's heels should be placed upon the man's forehead.

This will, first and foremost, open up your Yoni to the most exquisitely deep penetration. This is far deeper than either of the two previous advancements that have been made to the missionary position, and the depth of penetration that is afforded during sex is comparable to that provided by the Indrani position.

This means that the Nail Fixing position provides the deepest possible penetration out of all of the Kama Sutra positions. Additionally, the heels placed upon the man's forehead make him essentially subservient for the woman.

During the Toad, the most the woman can accomplish is gentle coaxing. However, in the Nail Fixing position the woman's dominance of the man is so complete that she can lay relaxed on her back and at the same time fully dictate practically every aspect of sex, from the speed to how the man is thrusting.

This is one of the most popular Kama Sutra positions, but bear in mind that it requires quite a bit of flexibility; so make sure you are physically able before you attempt this position.

The Crab Position

The crab position is again one of the more submissive positions for the woman. It involves a fair amount of flexibility, so keep this in mind before you attempt this position.

In order to perform the crab position, the woman has to lie on her back and tuck her legs into her chest. Her thighs need to be spread open just enough that the man has enough room to penetrate her Yoni, but not so much that her knees are no longer against her chest.

This position provides fairly deep penetration, but the true benefit of applying this position during sex is that it provides a significant amount of stimulation to both the clitoris as well as the G spot.

There are very few positions even in Kama Sutra that facilitate the stimulation of both of these major centers of female pleasure, so you can imagine just how effective this will be if you want to make your woman achieve orgasm as quickly as possible.

You can use this position in tandem with the Yawning position. In this position you will stimulate the woman's sexual hotspots making her more sensitive to sexual pleasure. When you change to the Yawning position you will be penetrating her deeply, creating a wonderful balance of deep penetration and superficial stimulation.

This is an extremely submissive pose, with the woman being completely pliable to the man's will. This makes it very compatible with the Yawning position, as both of these positions are going to allow the man to hold complete dominance over the woman.

If you alternate between these two poses, you are going to have to have your woman in the throes of orgasm in no time.

The Splitting Bamboo

This Kama Sutra sex position is quite different from all of the others, and will certainly be different from any kind of sex position you have ever heard of before. It is an extension of sorts to the Yawning position and is perhaps the submissive equivalent to the Nail Fixing position in that it offers advanced pleasure without making the man submissive to the woman.

What makes this sex position so unique is that it involves a range of motion that the woman will be conducting. The active aspect of this sex position makes it strikingly different from other sex positions which are usually static and do not involve any kind of motion whatsoever apart from the natural movements of sex.

In order to perform the splitting of the bamboo, the woman will first have to lie on her back. Once she is on her back, she will have to place a single leg on the man's shoulder, much as she would do in the Yawning position with both legs.

During the act of sex, however, the woman is supposed to alternate between each leg. This means that she will change the leg that is on the man's shoulders from right to left and back again constantly during sex.

The leg that is not on the man's shoulders can be folded with the knee pressed against his chest. The motion must remain constant throughout the lovemaking session unless the two partners change positions.

The benefit of this sex position lies purely in its movement. It does not provide deeper penetration than the Yawning position as the Nail Fixing position does. However, by constantly alternating which leg is placed upon the man's shoulder, the women will end up clenching her Yoni several times over the course of the sex.

Clenching the Yoni will greatly enhance the pleasure that is being derived from the thrusting. This is because whenever the woman clenches, her G spot ends up being pressed against the man's Lingam.

This means that whenever the man thrusts during the movement of her legs, he will brush against her G spot causing immense pleasure. In essence, the biggest benefit that this position provides is that it can make it a lot easier for the man to make the woman come, and the orgasm achieved can be extremely intense.

The Presser Position

This position is absolutely magnificent. It is an example of how the advanced techniques of Kama Sutra can introduce you to an entire world of pleasure that is hidden within your own body, providing you the key to unlocking these treasure troves of sexual passion.

In order to perform the presser position, the woman's back must be slightly raised off of the bed, floor, or whatever surface the two of you are having sex on. The back of her thighs must be pressed against his chest while her body is raised up, revealing her Yoni for him to penetrate.

The Presser Position is incredibly intense. It allows you to penetrate deeper than any other position. For all of the depth that the Indrani and Nail Fixing positions provide, they are in the end limited because they involve sex with the woman on her back.

The Presser Position, on the other hand, is not limited by this. Since the woman's back is raised, with her upper back resting on the head of the bed or a wall, the penetration can be even deeper than these two positions.

While you are having sex with you partner in this position, you are going to feel an incredible sense of connection and "oneness" with him or her. This connection stems from the depth of penetration that is occurring.

It is important to keep in mind that this position requires a significant amount of flexibility on the part of the woman.

Hence, it is highly recommended to practice yoga for a period of time before attempting it.

The Cow Position

This position may sound funny, but it is an intensely erotic one and can provide a great amount of deep penetration if you are willing to try it. It is also notable for being one of the wilder positions in the Kama Sutra.

In order to perform the Cow Position, the woman must face downwards and stand herself up on her hands and feet. This is similar to the "doggy style" position except for the fact that the woman will be on her feet rather than on her knees.

The man will be penetrating her from behind, and the way the body is positioned will allow him to penetrate with quite a bit of depth.

This position will also facilitate very rough sex, so if you want to simply let loose with your passion give this position a shot. Below is a picture of the advanced cow.

Supported Congress

This position is another one of the wilder positions that you can find in the Kama Sutra. Additionally, this position is quite easy to do and requires absolutely no flexibility whatsoever, which means that it can be easily practiced by even the most novice Kama Sutra practitioners.

This position involves the woman on her feet standing against the wall. This makes this the first position in this list that does not involve some form of lying down or prone position. The Supported Congress also distinguishes itself by being the only position where penetration is not recommended.

This is because penetration while the woman is in this position is quite difficult, to the point where actually doing it might end up forcing the woman to adopt a different position altogether.

Instead of penetrating, it is recommended that the man stimulate woman's clitoris with his Lingam. Doing so is a lot easier in this position than it would be in the majority of the other positions that have been described in the Kama Sutra.

Reverse Supported Congress

The Supported Congress is an excellent position, but it just does not provide enough excitement for people who are looking to have actual, penetrative sex while standing up.

This is why the reverse supported congress is such an excellent position. It is very simple to do, it essentially involves the woman standing up and facing the while, bending her back a little to make it easier for the man to penetrate her.

This position can be used if you and your partner want to start getting in touch with your wilder sides. It is an excellent position to use for rougher sex, but it does not provide very deep penetration nor does it provide any clitoral stimulation.

Suspended Congress

Following the kinkier and wilder theme that the previous few sex positions have followed, the Suspended Congress can provide you and your partner with a sexual experience that is slightly out of the ordinary and can really spice up your sex lives if the two of you are going through a sexual rut.

Performing the suspended congress is fairly easy to explain, but would be quite difficult to actually do in real life. It essentially involves picking the woman up, her wrapping her legs around you, and you penetrating her with the both of you standing up.

The true benefit that this position provides is that it is an improved version of the previous two positions. While both of the previous positions were quite kinky, one of them did not provide any opportunity for penetration, and the other did not provide the opportunity for deep penetration.

This position, on the other hand, can allow you to be rough and kinky with your partner and actually penetrate her as well. It is proof that Kama Sutra was a sexual text far ahead of its time with much to teach people about sexuality, especially considering how many kinky positions it has in it!

The Turning Position

This position involves a great deal of movement and is quite advanced. It essentially is the missionary position in reverse.

The girl remains on her back and the man is on top of her but his feet are on either side of her head.

This way requires you to be absolutely gentle while you are thrusting. This Kama Sutra position is quite exotic and the main benefit that it provides is that can bring a fair amount of excitement to your sex life. Hence, it is useful if you are going through a sexual rut.

The Chakra Position

This position involves extensive use of your Kundalini energy, which is mystical energy, locked within a dormant energy nexus at the base of your spine.

This Chakra Position is one of the most erotic positions in the Kama Sutra, but the real benefit of this position is that it is so incredibly intimate.

In order to perform this position, the man needs to sit on the bed with his legs spread open. The woman must sit down the same way, except her legs must be placed over his, locking the two partners together.

The two partners can then either place their hands on each other's shoulders or the man can place his hands on the woman's waist.

Penetration during this position is extremely intense, and the amount of intimacy the two partners can achieve is beyond anything that any other position can offer.

This incredible level of intimacy stems from the fact that both lovers are able to stare directly into each other's eyes. Additionally, this position is quite unique because it is the only position where neither partner is dominant over the other. Both partners are equal in the Chakra Position, which contributes to the feeling of harmony and oneness.

The Lotus Bloom

This position is a classic Kama Sutra position. It is perhaps the most distinctive position in this entire list, and the only one that can be seen and instantly recognized as being part of the ideology of Kama Sutra.

In order to perform this position, the man must first sit cross-legged. The woman must then sit in his lap, wrapping her legs around him.

Both partners are free to do whatever they want with their hands in this position, but it is recommended that the woman place her hands on the man's shoulders and the man place his hands on either the woman's waist or on the floor or surface that is behind him.

This position is firmly female dominant. It is, in fact, the first overtly female dominant position in this list. Unlike even the Nail Fixing position, where the dominance of the female depended on her controlling how the man performs during sex, in the Lotus Bloom the woman has the man directly under her power.

She can actually control how the sex is going instead of coaxing or forcing her partner to make love to her the way she wants him to.

The Kneeling Position

This position is very useful if you are a woman who is looking to be dominant during sex. In fact, this position is far more dominating for the woman than any other position in this list, even the Lotus Bloom position.

In this position, the woman is not just dominant. The man is submissive to her completely, with her dictating absolutely every aspect of the sex from the speed to the amount of power used down to even the amount of penetration that occurs, making this position unique even among the myriad Kama Sutra positions.

In this position, the man is to get on his knees in a way that his Lingam is free for the woman to use to penetrate herself.

The woman then crouches down onto the man's Lingam, guiding it into her using her hand. This way, the woman does not have to rely on the man for penetration, guiding him by telling him how deep to go and how fast to thrust.

The woman is completely in control of the thrusts in this position, making it a great option if you are a woman who likes to be dominant during sex.

The Leg Up Position

This is one of the wildest positions that are on this list, and is a more advanced form of the supported congress position that has been mentioned before.

It is more popular than the supported congress position because it involves a wall and allows the man to penetrate as well. Additionally, the woman tends to be extremely submissive while she is in this position.

In order to perform this position, the woman must have her back against the wall and place her legs upon the man's shoulders. This means that the man is going to support her entire bodyweight.

In many ways the Leg Up position is a combination of both suspended as well as supported congress. By bringing the best of both positions together, the Leg Up position becomes one of the most uninhibited sex positions that can be found in the Kama Sutra.

It should be noted that a significant amount of flexibility would be required from the woman in order to apply this position. Additionally, the man is going to have to have enough physical strength to fully support the weight of the woman throughout the duration of sex in order to make the position effective.

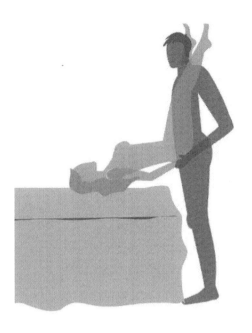

The Magic Mountain

This sex position can be considered a variation of the "doggy style" sex position but like so many other aspects of Kama Sutra, it is far better than anything the doggy style position could hope to provide.

The Magic Mountain involves the man standing behind the woman who would be kneeling on a slightly elevated service so that her backside is in line with the man's groin.

The man can penetrate the woman while she is on all fours, but then she must get up so that the man has to start thrusting upwards. This position is in many ways a far more advanced and erotic form of doggy style.

This is because it allows you to experience the same depth of penetration but also makes it a lot easier to caress and kiss your lover. You can also apply Kama Sutra techniques such as biting or one of the three kissing techniques while you are performing this technique.

The major benefit is that you can do all of these things while the woman's back is turned to you, adding a visceral edge to the sex that is just not present if you are doing it missionary style.

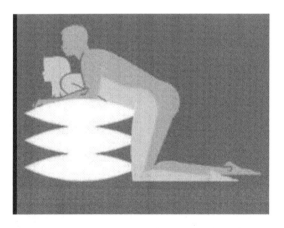

The Triangle

This position is quite unique because it allows the woman to be dominant and to command the pace of the thrusts all while more or less remaining on her back.

In this position, the man must get on his hands and knees above the woman. The woman will have to thrust upwards with her pelvis, making it easier for the man to penetrate her.

When she has been penetrated, either she can dominate and make the speed of the thrusting suit her preferences or the man and woman can thrust in tandem with each other.

The main benefit that this position provides is that it allows very deep penetration. This makes it easier for the man to ejaculate in a way that would facilitate conception.

Hence, if you are looking to conceive it is highly recommended that you try this position out. To make it easier and less physically exhausting the woman can put a pillow or two underneath her lower back so that she does not have to keep it elevated using just the strength of her muscles. Sex should ideally be a relaxing experience after all.

The Spoon

This is perhaps one of the most comfortable and least physically exhausting positions in this entire list. It involves practically no exertion of any kind, does not even require you to stand up, and even facilitates fairly deep penetration!

In order to apply this sex position, you and your partner will have to lie on your sides. The woman must have her back to the man, and the man can penetrate her if she sticks her backside out granting him easy access to her Yoni.

If you and your partner are really sleepy but really want to have sex, this is the position for you. It is very intimate as well because a lot of people tend to cuddle this way, which means that after both of you are finished you can simply go to sleep in that very same position.

It should be noted, however, that this position is not recommended for women who experience chronic back pain. The way this position is going to make the woman's back curve is not a healthy way for the spine to be if it is prone to getting damaged or aches due to prolonged stress that is placed on it over the course of the day.

Alternate Versions of the Spoon

There are two alternate versions of the spoon that you can also use during sex. The first of these is called the Ballerina.

In the Ballerina, the position remains the same except the man's legs are resting in between the woman's legs. This forces the man to pull his upper body away from the woman's upper body, creating a rather exotic angle in which the partners would be having sex.

The benefit of the Ballerina is that the penetration ends up being a lot deeper; although one drawback is that a lot of the intimacy of the Spoon position is lost since the man's upper body will be far away from the woman's.

Another variant of the Spoon is called the Curled Angel. In this position, the woman lies on her side and tucks her legs into her chest, sticking her backside out in order to facilitate penetration.

The man then wraps his arms around the woman, including her tucked in knees, and penetrates her. This position facilitates much deeper penetration and is both more intimate than the spoon position and makes the woman more submissive to the man during sex as well.

The Double Decker

This position is essentially a reverse lotus position except for a few major changes in the position the man is in.

In order to perform sex in this position, the man must sit down with his legs spread out and spread open in front of him. The woman will then turn her back to the man and sit down on his lap, her legs on top of his and her feet outside and next to his.

The woman is firmly dominant in this position, as she can decide the pace at which the sex will occur as well as the depth of penetration. It is recommended that both partners lean back during sex so that the woman is pressed up against the man, facilitating more intimacy.

The main benefit that can be derived from having sex in this position stems from the woman having her back facing the man. This boosts the dominance of the woman during sex, and having sex in this manner greatly heightens the sexual excitement in a unique way because the partners are not directly facing each other. It is recommended if you want a female dominant position that facilitates deep penetration.

The Crouching Tiger

This one is a classic "woman on top" position, and can allow you and your partner to have some truly great sex if it is applied properly.

In order to adopt the Crouching Tiger position, the man will need to lie on his back. This makes this the first position in this entire list where the man is doing so, and it will make him a lot more vulnerable and submissive to the woman facilitating a completely reversed sexual dynamic.

The man must spread his legs away from each other and the woman must stand atop him with one foot on each side of his hips. The woman must then crouch down onto him and then penetrate her Yoni with his Lingam herself.

It is recommended that the woman perform a rocking motion during sex, as this will greatly heighten the arousal during the act and is a movement that very few other positions facilitate.

It is recommended that you use this position if you want one where the woman is dominant. The man is completely submissive to the woman here, and she can control other aspects of sex as well such as the depth of penetration and the pace of the act.

The Elephant

The Elephant is rather submissive position for the woman and is very useful if the man is into positions where the woman is on her stomach. It is quite similar to the Cow Position in regards to how the man is going to penetrate, the only difference being that the woman will be on her stomach rather than her hands and knees.

Once the woman is on her stomach, the man will lie down on top of her, covering her body completely with his own. It is recommended that the woman spread her legs open with the man lying down between them in a way. This would make it easier for the man to penetrate the woman.

The benefit that you can get from this position is that it does not require much effort from the woman. If she is tired or unable to exert herself too much, this position allows her to be comfortable and let the man do all of the work for her.

However, this position does not facilitate much intimacy. It is recommended if you need some new sex positions to spice up your sex life but is not good as a regular sex position.

The Scissors

This position is quite kinky, and is also useful if you are part of a lesbian couple as it facilitates stimulation of both of your Yoni. It is one of the most unique and exciting positions among all of the positions mentioned within Kama Sutra.

In order to have sex in this position, both partners will have to be lying with the head next to each other's feet. They must then slip in between each other's legs, so that one leg is one each side of their partner's body and the Lingam has easy access to the Yoni.

The man must then penetrate the woman. Be careful during this position. If it is done improperly it could result in you or your partner sustaining injury.

However, if it is performed correctly in can bring a wildness to your sex life that is unparalleled. It is highly recommended that you use this position during sex if you are looking to spice up your nighttime trysts or are looking to reignite your sex life after a period of stagnation with your partner.

Chapter 6

A Kama Sutra Technique for Mind Blowing Female Orgasms

This technique is absolutely brilliant for pleasing your woman. If you are looking to make your woman happy, you probably know that the best way to do this would be to give her an orgasm.

By using this technique, you are not going to give her just the one orgasm; you are going to be able to give her several. The truly great thing about this technique is that the orgasms it gives your woman will be proper, full body orgasms that will leave her shaking with pleasure and will get you well into her good books!

The Massage

The first part of this orgasm technique involves a massage. It is essentially a standard massage, the only real difference is that it involves the use of oil and must be applied regularly over a period of time in order to become effective.

In order to perform this massage, you will first have to rub oil all over your woman's body. This can be any oil you prefer, but it is recommended that you get grape seed oil because it has various advantages as far as massage is concerned, such as being good for the woman's skin and being very light and easily absorbed.

The massage must focus on her entire body. The first stage essentially involves giving every part of her body a once over, rubbing across her body with firm hands to loosen up her muscles and get ready for the really deep massage.

Once her body is loosened up, you can apply deep pressure to certain areas. The areas you should be focusing on are the back and inside of her thighs, her lower back, her shoulders, and her backside as well as her breasts and Yoni in order to facilitate heightened stimulation while the actual technique is being applied.

The Technique

Bear in mind, you will have to perform the aforementioned massage for at least a week before you can apply this technique. In order for it to be effective the woman will have to be completely loose with absolutely no tension in her muscles.

Once you are sure that you have performed the massage regularly for an appropriate period of time, you can apply the technique. In order to do so, you must first make your woman lie down flat on her back with her legs spread slightly giving you access to her Yoni.

You must then penetrate her Yoni with your middle and ring fingers simultaneously. In order to do this properly, your palm must face upwards and your index and little fingers should be facing downwards and pressed flat against her buttocks in order to provide you with balance as you move onto the next step.

Once your fingers are inside her, you must jerk them upwards as vigorously as possible and continue doing so for around thirty seconds. There is no preamble to this, you are simply supposed to perform this act and jerk your hand upwards as forcefully as possible.

After continuing this motion for around thirty seconds, you can gently curl your fingers upwards in a "come hither" motion while stimulating her clitoris with your tongue.

Alternate between these two movements for a period of time. If your woman is comfortable and has been made loose and relaxed by the regular massages, she will be enjoying an intense orgasm in absolutely no time at all, an orgasm that will have her entire body shaking and contorting.

This movement might seem too rough, but it is actually not that violent for a part of the body that is designed to push miniature humans out of it!

Chapter 7
Beyond The Sex

If you've read this far, you will have picked up numerous techniques to make your sex life more fulfilling. You'll have learned about the stages of sex, how to make the most of foreplay, the most enjoyable sex positions, and also how to have mind-blowing orgasms. You should be more in tune with your body and your desires than you have ever been, and you should be much more aware of what makes for great sex. It's more than just instinct and basic levels of human existence – the Kama Sutra is a complete way of life, and if you can embrace that way of life, you will be much more fulfilled – sexually and in every other way.

Those who think the Kama Sutra is just about the sex are cherry picking from the book to get what they think they want from it. However, it is about much more than sex –

it's a lifestyle and a mindset, and to get the most benefit from the book, it's important to embrace all of the teachings, and work with all of the suggestions. When you look more deeply into the Kama Sutra, it's clear that many of the suggestions and instructions don't just apply to sexual matters. They can equally be applied to life outside the bedroom.

The literal translation of Kama Sutra is 'a treatise on pleasure,' but it does not refer exclusively to sexual pleasure. It's about living a good life, and embracing everything that life has to offer. The central character of the book is a man – a middle class man of means – but the advice in the book is aimed at both women and men. Both are expected to read it and gain from the knowledge. It points out that pleasure is not purely about the physical, but also about a meeting of minds. In other words, sex is not the only pleasure. Although it is enjoyable, it is so much more enjoyable when the partners are equal.

The Kama Sutra was put together in the third century AD by Vatsyayana, an Indian monk who compiled the writings of others into what essentially is a manual for living. Considering the time of compilation, it espouses some very liberated and even contemporary ideas. These are all the more surprising when you remember they date back to a time and a culture when the male was in the ascendant, and therefore the one to be pleased. Even today, India does not have such a liberal attitude to women as that put forward in the Kama Sutra.

Much of the narrative focuses on wealth rather than class, which is quite revolutionary in Indian literature, especially of that time. It's about culture, and the right way to behave, and that comes with money. The man about town who is the central character is fastidious about his personal hygiene, and appears to have no obvious means of income. He doesn't appear to work at any sort of job that will provide remuneration, although his days are ordered by routine.

The book seems to say that if you have money, you can live the dream, so as well as being a sex manual, it's an aspirational and inspirational guide as well, written in a way that is clearly aimed at empowering its readers, and demonstrating what they can achieve, as long as they follow the recommendations of the text. People who just hone in on the sexual passages miss the point of what the Kama

Sutra is all about. If you remember that it is often described as a scripture, you may get more of an idea of where the book is coming from. In many ways, it's a book of etiquette, describing what is expected of both men and women in prescribed situations.

There is also a lot of emphasis in the Kama Sutra on the body-mind-spirit holistic connection, with advice on foods to eat, and remedies to try if there are physical or emotional problems. Today, that sort of thing is taken for granted, but around 1700 years ago, it would have been revolutionary thinking.

These days, reviewers describe the Kama Sutra as a self help book, although they also say that it's not likely to improve your sex life, so it may be somewhat confusing for modern readers, who pick up the book and battle through one of the various translations with the express intention of doing exactly that. However, there are other things that you can take from the Kama Sutra, which will enhance your life and carry over into the realms of sex and pleasure, but to gain full benefit from these things, you need to engage fully with the Kama Sutra mindset, and recognize why the book can be so helpful in all aspects of your life, not just the sexual.

When you can adjust to this new level of thinking, you will understand more fully exactly what the Kama Sutra is offering. It's not just sex – it's life fulfillment in all its aspects. Sex is just a small part of it. Rethinking your attitudes to life – including the life you share with your partner – is the main message of the book, and if you read it at a deeper level, you will be able to connect with that message and reap the benefits. Surprisingly, since the Kama Sutra's main character is a man, there is a lot about women in there, and keeping your woman happy in and out of the bedroom. In the next chapter we'll take a look at the Kama Sutra mindset regarding women.

Veronica Baruwal

Chapter 8
The Kama Sutra's Ideal Woman

The attitude to women in the Kama Sutra is something of a paradox, because it combines traditional third century Eastern attitudes with incredibly modern thinking. Many people don't really 'get' what it's trying to say, and tend to skim over it and just concentrate on the sexual advice. That's a real pity, because the Kama Sutra has some good advice on Dharma – virtuous living – and a lot of it is still relevant today, almost 1700 years after it was compiled. Some of the writings provide a unique insight into the way women were perceived at the time, and they may also give pause for thought, because looking at this from a modern, Western viewpoint, some of the ideas and ethics espoused in the Kama Sutra seem very strange.

You need to remember that pretty much all of the writings are linked to the ideal of Dharma, which is one of the four purusharthas, or main goals of life, according to various Indian philosophies. The four goals are:

Dharma – Virtuous living, and the most important of the four. It's tied in with reincarnation, and working off bad karma from previous lives. Basically, it's atoning for previous sins by living by the rules in the present life. When this has been achieved, the goal of Moshka can be attained. Therefore, the older a person is, the more important Dharma becomes.

Artha – Material prosperity, which is particularly important for a ruler, who must guide, govern, and protect his people. This also includes the acquisition of friends, as well as material possessions such as land and money. Artha in its finest form also includes the protection of that prosperity, which means looking after your land, your animals, your business, your family, and your friends.

Kama – Physical desire and pleasure, and the least important of the four goals. The pleasure is based on the five senses, so as well as sexual desire, there are other sensory pleasures to be explored and enjoyed.

Moshka – Afterlife liberation, which comes when the soul is free from earthly concerns. This happens when someone has worked out all their karma and can escape from the cycle of birth and death and move on to eternal life.

Of these four goals, the first three are concerned with earthly life, and when you remember that virtuous living is the most important, while physical desire is least important, it gives you a clue to the true mindset behind the Kama Sutra. While desire is acknowledged and explored, the Kama Sutra is not simply the ancient sex manual that many people assume it is, and it is certainly not a blueprint for tantric sex. There is a lot more to it than that.

The instructions for men dealing with women are quite exhaustive and specific. There are certain women it is okay to mix with socially and sexually, while other women are off limits. And although the importance of Dharma and virtuous living is repeatedly emphasized, there are numerous occasions where adultery is justified, condoned, or even applauded. As long as the man has sexual congress with the ideal woman as defined in the Kama Sutra, neither of them are considered to be sinning, even if one or both of them is married.

The Different Kinds of Women in the Kama Sutra

There are different terms for the various types of women in the Kama Sutra. The expectations from the woman regarding social and sexual behavior would be understood from the term applied to her.

Charshani – Basically a high-class courtesan, who would be expected to pleasure the most important men in her society, from the king down. So, officers in the military or elders of the village could request the favors of a Charshani and she would be obliged to comply. Charshanis would have been very attractive women, both aesthetically and sexually, and although they were compelled to grant sexual favors when asked, they would also be respected.

Devi – This is the Sanskrit word for goddess, which would be used exclusively to address female members of the royal family or the aristocracy. A man might also use it as a term of endearment to his lover, but only in private, and most usually when they were having sex, or during foreplay.

Doodi – This is a facilitator, a matchmaker who plays Cupid between a man and a woman, or in more unpleasant circumstances, she will help a woman to escape from an unworthy or unkind man. Broadly, the term means 'messenger.'

Nayika – A romantic heroine and the object of men's desire and fantasies. Nayikas fall into three main types – virgins, women who have been married, or public women who may be distinguished from the rest by being called a Ganika. She will be a respected, learned woman, who is accomplished in all the arts expected to be learned by a woman of quality, as well as all the sensual arts needed to please her man.

Tapasi – A woman who lives a virtuous life in the service of God and has renounced the pleasures of the flesh, the western equivalent of a Nun.

Vatsala – A married woman who has given birth to children. She would be respected for her fertility and her knowledge and experience.

All these women would be expected to have a well rounded education, in all the practicalities of life, social niceties, and of course, how to please their men. The list of accomplishments a girl needed is exhaustive and intimidating to modern eyes, but it also opens an intriguing window on how life was lived in the third century, and what was considered important.

The Kama Shastra

There are 64 practices known as the Kama Shastra, which women were expected to study and become proficient in, as well as learning the sexual practices listed and described in detail in the Kama Sutra. A girl could learn by independent study, and also by example and teaching from trusted female friends and relatives. The important points are that this study took place in private, and the tutor should be a trusted and respected woman, preferably one who was already married. It wasn't necessary for the teacher to be of a different generation either – in fact an older sister is a highly recommended teacher, since she 'can always be trusted.'

The exhaustive list is quite a tall order for anyone, since it includes singing, dancing, and playing a musical instrument – and combining the three together! And she should be able to play a recognizable tune on glasses filled to varying levels with water. The lady also needs to be able to act on a stage, and mimic other people, as well as being able to fight with a sword and a bow and arrow, and play word games and mind games successfully. She should also be versed in the art of tattooing. In other words, the Eastern lady was a home entertainment center in all senses of the word!

The Kama Shastra lady should be able to talk to the animals – as well as teaching parrots and starlings to talk back. And she needed to be adept in the arts of cock fighting and ram fighting, as well as being able to make and take bets on the proceedings, because the accomplished lady was no stranger to gambling.

The well brought up Eastern lady should also be able to make her own clothes, and make animals and birds out of yarn and wool, as well as tassels and fringes to adorn clothing and home furnishings. Our lady needed to know how to make and arrange rugs and pictures and soft furnishings to look comfortable and aesthetically pleasing. As if that wasn't enough, she was also expected to know how to inlay stained glass into the floor of her home. And she needed to have some knowledge of gardening, carpentry, architecture, and building.

On top of all that, she had to be a wizard in the kitchen, cooking and making drinks from lemonade to spirits. Everything had to be just the right color and flavor too, or she would have found herself in trouble!

On a more cerebral level – though heaven knows when she would have had time for it – the well brought up young lady was expected to write poetry, read books, draw and paint, and practice magic and sorcery. All this on top of making herself desirable by making perfumes and jewelry, coloring her teeth, hair, and nails, and making floral head dresses and hair decorations.

All this takes some getting your head around, because on the one hand, it seems that women were prized for their brains and accomplishments, so one could hardly say they were simply sex objects and breeding machines. The Eastern woman of the third century must have been intelligent, attractive, practical, and entertaining, but it seems she was also expected to run the household with virtually no help from her partner.

The main male character in the book – the wealthy man about town - would spend a lazy morning, rising late, then having a bath and attending to his own ablutions before breakfasting and then going out to meet friends and attend to his business. Since this business was usually accomplished without having to do any manual work or even break a sweat, it was hardly exacting.

So then, the ideal woman according to the Kama Sutra really needed to be Superwoman in order to attract herself a mate or be the object of desire of kings, princes, and leaders. Even then, there were some types of women that men were advised to steer clear of, however accomplished they may be. In the next chapter, we'll examine the attitude to different types of women in third century India.

Chapter 9
What is Desirable and Undesirable in a Woman

These days, a husband or lover who is having relationship problems may lash out and say 'Mother always warned me about women like you.' However, it's not a modern thing, because the Kama Sutra contains lots of detailed advice on the type of women who should be avoided at all costs, women who would make suitable friends, but not necessarily lovers, and women it's okay to commit adultery with. Yes, in the Kama Sutra mindset, there are so many instances where it's okay for a man and a woman who are married to other people to sleep together; it's almost an Adulterer's Charter. Apparently, if you have an affair or just a brief sexual interlude for the right reasons with the right woman, it's not sinful at all.

To modern Western sensibilities, this smacks of hypocrisy, but to the compilers and original readers of the Kama Sutra, it would be seen as virtuous living and conducting yourself according to the standards of your peers. This is also tied in with the protection of your prosperity and the enjoyment of sensory pleasure – it's not as black and white as simply sleeping with another man's wife, and this is a difficult concept for people to grasp today. That's probably why people tend to skim over these sections without giving them too much thought. It all seems very archaic and contrived to modern minds.

Women to Avoid

Before a man could be friends – or friends with benefits – with the right type of woman, he needed to be very clear on the kind of woman who was undesirable, and the Kama Sutra is very clear on this. Women to avoid included lepers, lunatics, those who are disgraced or cannot keep secrets, someone who is a close relation or personal friend, or a religious woman – in other words a Tapasi.

Morals and personal attractiveness come into it as well. A woman whose skin is too light or too dark should be avoided, as should any woman who is unhygienic and has body odor, or a woman who is blatant in her desire for sexual intercourse. Just as women are taught the things they need to know to become desirable in private, so sex is a private matter. One could talk about it generally, but not about specifics between couples, or particular desires.

Aside from lepers and lunatics – which is more about self preservation than anything else – these strictures can be construed as good advice for modern men all over the world who are looking for an ideal partner with whom they can enjoy a fulfilling intimate relationship. It may have been written 1700 years ago, but it's still very relevant today.

Very close relations and personal friends are not the best candidates for lovers and life partners, and that works for both men and women. On one hand, you may feel that because you already know each other and each other's likes, dislikes, and habits so well, it's a great foundation for a lasting relationship. To some extent, this is true, but there is a certain danger in knowing too much about someone's history before embarking on intimacy. You may subconsciously try to change them to conform to your perception of an ideal partner, and while this can happen in any relationship, someone who is a close relative or friend is likely to be particularly wounded by such behavior because they will assume that you know and accept their perceived faults. Trying to change their personality under such circumstances is likely to be seen as disrespectful and a betrayal of trust.

Additionally, when you know someone's history really well, you also know stuff they'd rather was forgotten. When you have a major disagreement, some of that stuff may be brought out as a weapon. It's not nice and it's not fair, but because people are only human, it's the sort of thing they do when they want to win an argument. However, the main reason for avoiding an intimate relationship with a close relative or friend – whether a man or a woman – is that should the relationship founder, then the family relationship or friendship may never be the same again. While everyone needs someone to love and to share their life with, you also need good friends and supportive family members who know you really well, and starting a sexual relationship could ruin those special friendships.

When it comes to people who can't keep secrets or are blatant about their desire for sex, that's still a good reason to avoid a close relationship with them. It all comes down to trust, and if you can't trust your partner to keep your secrets or be faithful, you don't really have the foundation for a successful long-term relationship.

These days, the guidance about people whose skin is too dark or too light and people who don't keep themselves clean is pretty much redundant, and has no place in the modern Kama Sutra mindset. People are much more fastidious about personal hygiene, and can afford the things they need to keep themselves clean and fresh, and most people do not discriminate against potential partners on the grounds of color. Love is love, and attraction is about the person they happen to be, not the color of their skin.

Women as Friends

The Kama Sutra is pretty definite on the type of women a man should count amongst his friends. It's also clear that it's okay to have friends of the opposite sex, which was pretty revolutionary thinking way back in the third century.

The thinking was that to really be able to please your woman sexually, you needed to understand how her mind worked, and the best way to do that was to have female friends with whom you were not intimately involved, to improve your understanding of women. That's a very modern outlook – lots of people these days have friends of the opposite sex, and nobody thinks there's anything wrong with it. Of course the modern trend is also for 'friends with benefits,' where your friends are also occasional, no strings attached, sexual partners. While the Kama Sutra counsels against sex with friends, it's clear from some of the exclusions – which will be examined more closely in the next chapter – which it's not expressly forbidden in the pursuit of Dharma.

The types of women who would make suitable friends for the young man about town include childhood friends, people with similar likes, dislikes, and disposition, children who have been brought up together, such as cousins and the children of neighbors or family servants, and fellow students. Basically anyone you have history or interests in common with, which is still a firm foundation for friendship these days.

These friends should be honest, and consistent in their behavior and morals. They should want to help you achieve your goals, without being envious of your successes, and they should be discreet with your secrets but firm enough to give advice when they feel you need it. They should also be loyal to you, and not betray your trust with others. All this is pretty much a blueprint for a successful modern day friendship, isn't it? Some things never change – they are universal, and the qualities of friendship are numbered amongst those universalities.

Adultery – or Just a 'Resort?'

As mentioned before, in the Kama Sutra mindset, it's perfectly fine to sleep with another man's wife under certain conditions. Most of these conditions have something to do with revenge and self-preservation, as well as the obvious motive of enjoying another woman. Again, this seems strange to modern sensibilities – particularly as the writers and compilers of the Kama Sutra refer to intercourse with another woman as 'resorting' to her. There's a bit of detail about women of higher castes, and those who are lawfully married, but if they've been twice married, or enjoyed by other men previously, it's okay for the man about town to enjoy them too.

Basically, it was deemed okay to sleep with another man's woman purely for pleasure without compromising Dharma, as long as other conditions were in place. For example, if she was married to the man's enemy, she was fair game, or if she'd been spreading her favors freely before he met her. Strangely, if the woman's husband wasn't too keen on someone, it was okay for another man to sleep with her, so that she'd influence him in their favor.

Although according to the Indian philosophy resorting to another man's wife was supposed to be purely for Kama – or pleasure – the prevailing view was that it was okay for the man to do it if it would bring him extra wealth or advantages, since that was fulfilling the objective of Artha, which is the accumulation of wealth and the protection of property and reputation. That's why if a woman knew something detrimental about a man, he was quite likely to sleep with her to keep her quiet.

So effectively, all the advantages of adultery accrued to the man – although presumably the woman got some pleasure out of it too. Possibly you could argue that it is still the case these days, although the Kama Sutra idea of adultery was more of a one-off, pleasurable act, which, if undertaken with the right person for the right reasons, would not mark either of the couple as sinners.

Modern extramarital lovers seem to go in for affairs rather than one night stands, and are usually more circumspect, because they don't have the comfort of knowing that, according to the Kama Sutra, it's okay to commit adultery. On the other hand, the mere fact that the affair is clandestine and forbidden lends an extra frisson of passion, and the people concerned probably feel they have some justification for their actions, so maybe it isn't so different after all.

While some of the ideas about women in the Kama Sutra seem outdated and even outlandish at first glance, on reappraisal and deeper analysis, a lot of the thinking is also relevant today. That suggests that when it comes to attitudes to women and sex, there really is nothing new under the sun!

Veronica Baruwal

Chapter 10
The Kama Sutra and Tantric Sex

While modern commentators insist that the Kama Sutra is not an instruction manual for tantric sex, and this is indeed a valid point, many of the ideas espoused in the writings have a lot in common with the teachings of the Tantra. In both the Kama Sutra and tantric practices, the satisfaction of the woman is just as important as the satisfaction of the man – if not more so – and the woman is often revered as some sort of goddess. There are also many sexual positions in the Kama Sutra which are ideal for tantric sex, so one can't help but think that the writers and compilers were at least familiar with tantric teachings, and incorporated these ideas into the magnum opus that is the Kama Sutra.

There are hundreds of sexual positions – many more than are actually listed in the Kama Sutra - but not all of them will be suitable for tantric sex, for a number of reasons. Tantric sex engenders a deeper level of intimacy, and relies on lots of eye content and relaxed enjoyment of each other's bodies. It's not about the race to orgasm – it's about the whole sensual journey, and orgasm isn't a requirement every time. As long as the couple enjoy intense, pleasurable sensations throughout the experience, it's not essential to come to orgasm. That said, many practitioners of tantric sex do experience one or more orgasms, but it's not the true aim of the game.

Sexual positions for tantric sex should allow the partners to touch and be intimate with each other, since these are major requirements of tantric sex. Also, the couple should be able to breathe correctly throughout, so some of the more athletic, difficult to achieve, and hold positions will clearly be right off the radar.

Sitting sexual positions, especially where the partners are facing each other and entwined, are particularly good for tantric sex, and there are a number of those in the Kama Sutra, and in many Indian writings and pieces of art and sculpture. Comfort and relaxation are essential to allow the energy to build gradually so that both partners can take full sensory advantage of it, so that will naturally exclude some positions.

Because tantric sex sessions can go on for much longer than regular sex sessions, it's best to avoid anything that's very energetic or extremely athletic. This can make the breathing difficult to maintain, and also, you may find yourself more focused on maintaining the position and your balance, than concentration on your partner and your pleasure. The point of tantric sex is total concentration on the moment and on each other, and you need to remember this when considering appropriate sex positions. These are some of the best positions for tantric sex, taking into account the basic principles. Some come directly from the Kama Sutra, while others are clearly inspired by it.

Yab Yum

Yab Yum is a basic position of the Tantra that is often used in a non-sexual manner, to make eye contact or practice breathing exercises, or simply to meditate and connect on an emotional level. It's the embodiment of the male-female connection and union. However, it's also a great position for sex, since it ticks the major tantric sex boxes of eye contact, intimacy, and being able to explore each other's bodies. It's also a slow build up position. The position most similar to it that is described in the Kama Sutra is the Lotus Blossom.

He sits on the floor, cross-legged, possibly on a large cushion or a beanbag for increased comfort. She then climbs on his lap and wraps her legs around him, so they are pretty much intertwined. The beauty of this position is that the couple maintain close contact, and are able to look deep into each other's eyes, as well as having plenty of opportunities for kissing and licking, and touching each other all over the body.

Yab Yum also aligns the couple perfectly for kissing, touching, and rubbing against one another. He can gently rock, to increase friction and stimulate the G-spot. You could also try this position on a nice deep armchair or couch. This is a good position to slow down the man's ejaculation too, because he can rest and breathe to bring it all back under control and extend the intimate experience.

For the woman, there's a closeness and intimacy in the Yab Yum position that heightens the whole encounter. She can experience deep penetration, and can also squeeze on his penis (called the lingam in Tantra, so that's the term we'll use for it here) inside her yoni (vagina). It's a position that allows for the generation and exchange of sexual energy that is so important in tantric sex.

After orgasm – which is often simultaneous in the Yab Yum position – the couple can stay connected, and possibly enjoy more orgasms, just by focusing on their close physical connection. She can hold him inside her, and use her pelvic floor muscles to hold his lingam in place for hours of pleasure. It's the classic tantric sex position, and even if you do not practice tantric sex, it's something you should try at least once.

The Butterfly

This is one of the more famous of the Kama Sutra sex positions, and it's also ideally suited to tantric sex, which kind of strengthens the case that the writers of the Kama Sutra were also familiar with the teachings of the Tantra, and incorporated some of those ideas within it. She lies on the edge of a table, counter, couch, or bed and he kneels or stands in front of her for penetration. She then rests her legs on his shoulders.

The Butterfly allows for regular tantric breathing, plenty of eye contact, and also plenty of touching and caressing, although kissing is pretty much impossible in this position. However, he can kiss and lick her legs and feet. You should both be able to synchronize your movements and your breathing in this position.

Change up the Butterfly by bringing your legs together on one shoulder, rather than spreading them. That will make his lingam feel larger inside you, and put more pressure on the G-spot. And there are various variations of the Butterfly position, which are reminiscent of Yab Yum, with intertwined legs. All in all, the Butterfly position is just made for tantric sex, and it's good for slow, sensual movements too. Whether or not you are into tantric sex, it's good to try at least one variation of this position.

Don't ask how it got its name though – nobody seems to know for sure! One suggestion is that the action of the woman's legs during sex are reminiscent of the movement of the butterfly's wings in flight. Fanciful? Yes, but it's quite a charming thought, don't you think?

Karma Tidal Wave

This position is another one that ticks all the tantric sex boxes, so to speak. It's another face-to-face position, allowing for close intimacy and eye contact. He lies on his back, and she straddles him as he enters her. Now they should line up the hips together, synchronizing the breathing as she slides up and down along him, rubbing her clitoris along his pubic bone, keeping up friction and making for deep, intense orgasms.

This tidal wave can also be used as a rear entry position, with her face down and him on top. When you have progressed along your personal tantric path, this position can be used for anal penetration, or awakening the root, as it is known in the Tantra. It's an advanced technique, requiring a lot of love and trust in your partner, as well as a sensual flow of sexual energy, ·so it's not something newcomers to tantric sex should be considering.

Both versions of this position allow for connection after orgasm, which is another important part of the tantric sex experience. And the continued connection often leads to more orgasms – that's the true beauty of tantric sex.

The Sidewinder

This position is another position that seems to be just made for tantric sex. Basically, it's a side position, where you are very close together, face-to-face. It's a position that's made for slow, steady, sensual build up to orgasm, and that's what tantric sex is all about. The position gives you the opportunity for lots of eye contact and intimacy, and allows you to use your hands to stroke, caress, and stimulate each other further.

Lie on your sides, facing each other, and as she lifts her upper leg and he enters her, she drapes it across him. Move slowly and sensually, matching your breathing and enjoying each sensation fully. She can rest her feet against a wall or headboard to give her more leverage and control of movement, and wrapping her leg around his torso will increase the sensations inside her, as well as giving him more range of movement. The sidewinder also allows your man more range of movement if you relax your grip on his torso.

All the positions detailed here are suitable for those practicing tantric sex, and also people who just want to get more out of their sexual experiences and enjoy deeper, more satisfying orgasms. In the Kama Sutra, on the section dealing with intercourse, great emphasis is placed on staying closely connected, even after orgasm and ejaculation. Even if the connection doesn't lead to further intercourse, it is a deep form of intimate contact. Such connection after intercourse is also recommended in tantric teaching, because both mindsets are focused on enjoying each other and achieving satisfaction, not just having sex, however mind-blowing it may be.

Padlock

This pose is extremely sexy as it helps both him and her look at each other while remaining connected. That helps them make eye contact and entice each other with sexual expressions. For the padlock, she has to lie down on a flat surface that will help him access her easily. She has to lie on her back and support herself by placing her elbows on the table. Her yoni should be lined against his penis. He can then enter her. His hands are free to do whatever he wants to do or what she wants him to do. Seeing her flipping her head and hair back and forth will drive him crazy and help him perform better.

Double Decker

This is one of those poses that give her the chance to dominate. So those looking to take charge must try this pose out. It also gives him a clear view of what's going on, which will make him very happy and aroused. To perform this pose, he should sit on the bed with his legs under his body. You can sit on the bed or the table to add an element of risk. She should sit on his lap facing the other side and have her legs on either side of him. She must then move herself up and down and please herself and her partner.

Mermaid

The mermaid is a variation of the butterfly. As we saw in the butterfly, she has to sleep on a bed or a table. She must place a pillow below her butt so that she allows very little gap in between her legs. She must lift her leg 90 degrees into the air. He then holds her legs or wraps his hands around her legs and enters her tight grip. This pose will prove to be extremely satisfying for both him and her.

Hot Seat

The hot seat is a lot like the mermaid but will give you more pleasure. The hot seat is where he sits on the bed with his legs under his butt and spaced at a distance. The girl sits in between her legs and faces the other way. She sits on his lap quite close to his body such that their thighs and upper bodies touch. She then moves up and down. This motion is sure to set the right mood and the man will go crazy with pleasure!

Pretzel

This is often regarded as the most picturesque pose as the couple will resemble a pretzel when they get into it. It starts with both kneeling on the floor and facing each other. The two must kneel down very close to each other almost falling on one another. The girl then lifts her left leg and places it next to the man's right and the right leg next to the man's right. It can sound a bit complicated but really is not. Once you do, the two of you can hold hands and look into each other's eyes while going through the intercourse.

Rowboat

The rowboat is a great pose for both him and her. It is only possible to perform this pose by sitting on a chair that is capable of bending back. Once the man sits, he bends backwards and has her sit over his penis. She then moves up and down and pleasures both herself and her partner. He can place his hands below her butt to support her movement.

Lap dance

The lap dance is a very sexy pose and sure to leave you extremely pleased. It starts with him sitting on a comfortable chair and her sitting on his lower stomach. She then raises her legs in the air and places them over his shoulders. He then adjusts her lower body to match with his penis and enters her. This can be a very fulfilling pose that is sure to leave you feeling great about yourself.

Spread

The spread is a basic tantric pose but one of the most sought after. Both he and she will have an extremely pleasurable experience while performing it. It starts with her sleeping on the bed or couch and spreading her legs as much as possible. He then stands in front of her and enters her. Both will have a very pleasurable experience taking this exercise up. There is nothing too tough about it and both will have a great time looking at each other's bodies and faces.

G-force

The G-force is where he has more control over her. She lies down on the bed and he kneels in front of her. He then pulls her close and lifts her legs in the air. He can enter her mid-air, which is sure to drive both crazy. He can also choose to pull her towards him and push her away to enhance the experience.

Intertwining

The intertwine looks a little difficult but is in fact quite easy. It starts with both sitting on the floor facing each other. The guy then places both his feet around her to embrace her with his legs. She then lifts her legs and inserts them under his underarms. This creates a picturesque pose.

Both the Kama Sutra and the Tantra teach that the best sex comes from taking your time and concerning yourself more with your partner's pleasure than your own. They also advise that you should enjoy extended foreplay and experiment with different sexual positions until you find the ones that increase pleasure and deliver the most intense orgasms.

Chapter 11
The Vital Components of the Kama Sutra Mindset

As has already been mentioned, the Kama Sutra is not just about sex – that's how people tend to perceive it these days – largely thanks to the emphasis on the sex positions and the detailed descriptions of intercourse and foreplay. It offers insights into male-female relationships that may seem archaic at first, but if you stop and think about the reasoning behind the words, a lot of it still makes perfect sense today. It's about respecting other people, but above all, respecting yourself and your body, so that you can enjoy fulfilling intimate relationships.

Kama Sutra is a whole lifestyle for both men and women—not necessarily a belief system, but a way of living so that you get the most out of life in all ways, not just sexually. Like numerous other Eastern philosophies, it is aimed at achieving enlightenment, and the path to this can be travelled in a sexual or non-sexual way, or indeed a combination of the two. Here, then, are the things you need to address to pave the way to the authentic Kama Sutra mindset.

Breathe Right

Breathing is something everybody just does without giving it a second thought – it's automatic. If you don't breathe, you lose consciousness, and if you continue not to breathe, you die from lack of oxygen to the brain, so the body makes sure this doesn't happen. However, Kama Sutra, like many Eastern philosophies, relies on the union of mind, body, and spirit, and to achieve this, you need to be in tune with your breathing.

Aside from the sexual aspect, deep breathing relaxes the mind and the body and delivers extra oxygen to the muscles and organs, so you feel more at ease and supple. A popular breathing exercise is to breathe in deeply through your nose, taking the breath right down into your belly, then expel the breath through the mouth. That one can actually lower blood pressure, believe it or not, and seeing as relaxation is at the heart of great sex, you can see why the Kama Sutra – and also the teachings of the Tantra - recommends conscious breathing, rather than purely instinctive breathing.

Deep breathing can also prolong sex and stave off orgasm. At the approach of orgasm, the breathing naturally gets a little ragged, but if you can control it by breathing deeply and calmly, the urge to climax will subside, and you'll be able to carry on. When you do eventually have your orgasm, it will be much more intense. That works for both men and women, and it's a particularly useful skill to acquire if you're a man and you have a problem with premature ejaculation. Often it can be controlled and your staying power increased by using the correct breathing techniques.

Practice breathing in, and down past the lungs into the abdomen, then hold it for a second and exhale, taking slightly longer to expel the breath than you did to inhale. This will ensure your body is emptied of stale air and filled with fresh, oxygenated breath. It may feel rather strange at first, and you could experience a slight feeling of light-headedness, but once you've mastered the skill of deep breathing you will look and feel much healthier and energetic. And that makes for great sex, and great everything really.

Maintain Eye Contact

Have you ever noticed how turned on you get when you're making love and you hold eye contact? Well, Kama Sutra philosophy encourages maintaining eye contact in order to build intimacy. It's more than just eye contact though – it's prolonged, intimate, soul gazing eye contact that is at the same time energizing and scary. Normally, people don't maintain eye contact for more than a few seconds, so it can be challenging to hold that gaze for a length of time that could be construed as a hostile and aggressive stare by many people. However, it is a skill that can be learned, and it will enhance your sexual pleasure when you have developed it as a couple. It really will bring a new dimension to your shared intimacy.

To do it right, you need to be relaxed, and comfortable both in mind and body. Sit facing each other, as close as you can get. Close your eyes, think calm thoughts, and then open them and concentrate on your partner. Remember it's a soulful, intensive gaze – not a competition to see who breaks the stare first. You need to get that straight in your mind before you even start.

Take it Slowly

Great, satisfying sex is all about becoming absorbed in one another, and paying homage to each other's bodies as you get to know each other completely. It's not supposed to be a 'rip your clothes off' raunch, but it is supposed to be satisfying at a deep emotional and physical level. It's also not a race to the finish – in other words, orgasm. It's a journey through sensuality until you both reach the stage where you need to release your feelings and let them flow and combine. Then the orgasm will be all encompassing for both of you.

Learn to tease by stroking, kissing, licking, gently biting, and slapping, and enjoying each other's bodies and the sensations you produce. The Kama Sutra also recommends slapping your genitals against your partner's to intensify your pleasure. That said, it's not just about stimulating and touching the genital area, although there are specific massages you can use to intensify the pleasure. These are called Lingam and Yoni massages, after the Sanskrit words for the penis and the vagina. The massages are not intended to bring the partners to orgasm, although this may, and does, happen. It's more a question of total relaxation, and part of the slow but satisfying progress of truly fulfilling sex.

The Kama Sutra also stresses the importance of extended foreplay. This is tied in with the Kama mindset that the woman must be totally ready for intercourse before it happens. She should be so ready for it that she is already self-lubricating and parting her legs ready for her man to enter her, and foreplay, teasing, touch, and everything that goes with it are all intended to bring the female to a pitch of high arousal, to the point where she is physically trembling with anticipation. Only then, when both partners are excited and ready to fully enjoy each other, can mutually fulfilling lovemaking take place.

Respect and Love Your Body and Your Partner

Many Eastern philosophies view men and women as divine beings – in other words, gods and goddesses – and the body as a temple to be respected and revered. So Kama Sutra and tantric sex isn't just about the sex – performance and action – it's about the lifestyle, and having respect and love for both yourself and your partner. Sex is just another form of energy, and a sacred energy at that, so to completely embrace the Kama Sutra mindset, you may need to review and most likely change your whole ingrained attitude towards sex and love. Fortunately, this is a skill you can learn if you really want to.

Thinking of yourself as a god or goddess may seem fanciful at first, but it's a good way to build self-esteem and confidence, and the more confident you are, the more relaxed and happy you will be. Those who followed the recommendations of the Kama Sutra – particularly women – were expected to be accomplished in many arts and skills – not just the arts of love, and accomplishment invariably builds confidence. This in turn makes you more receptive to love, and more adventurous when it comes to sex.

The good news is, these lifestyle and attitude changes are not difficult to make, and they can make a difference to your sex life and your life with your partner almost immediately. You'll see results the minute you become conscious of your breathing, because you will be drawing more oxygen into your body to circulate to the muscles and organs. And when you get to grips with the rather challenging skill of deep soul gazing through extended eye contact, you will learn more about your partner and yourself.

Combine all this with a healthy eating plan, as another way to worship your body as a temple, and take the time to do some yoga and pelvic floor exercises to tone your body and increase your sexual pleasure. Kama Sutra and tantric sex is all about the holistic union of mind, body, and spirit, not just the coming together of the genitals in order to reach orgasm. If anything, in the Kama Sutra mindset, the orgasm itself is a pleasant bonus, rather than the main event and the sole object of the exercise.

Obviously, the more you practice these techniques, the more naturally they will come to you, and the more fulfilling your sex life will be, as well as your general life, because this kind of sex is healthy, satisfying sex that frees and stimulates the mind and the body, making you more aware of and in tune with both your own body and your partner's. And that is the heart and soul of the Kama Sutra mindset, distilled into a single sentence. It's an objective well worth working towards, and it's within everyone's reach.

Veronica Baruwal

Chapter 12
Female Masturbation Importance and Tips

As was mentioned earlier, the Kama sutra promotes masturbation as it helps improve people's sexual pleasure. There is nothing more enticing than being led during sex and if you tell your partner what makes you happy then the two of you will have heightened pleasure.

Women masturbate for a whole host of reasons that are apart from knowing oneself better. Some women masturbate to relieve themselves from period pain and cramps. Others do it to reel in mental peace and fall asleep. Most women start to masturbate at the time of puberty, as their sexual instincts will kick in. Some will not know how to pleasure themselves and begin experimenting. It will take around a year for a woman to perfect her style and pleasure herself thoroughly.

Method:

There are many ways in which a woman can masturbate and depends on what pleases her most. You can pick from three distinct styles that are as follows:

• Stoking the clitoris: The clitoris is a very sensitive part of the vagina and is located above the vulva. Most women prefer to stroke their clitoris repeatedly to pleasure themselves.

• Rubbing the labia: The labium is located just below the clitoris and is like a hood. This is also just as sensitive as the clitoris and so some women will prefer to stroke it.

• The third method is to insert an object into the vulva. This is on par with having intercourse as the penis is replaced by an object of similar shape.

• Some women make use of a vibrator to place over their clitoris as it helps in stimulating and arousing them.

- It is also possible for her to generate an orgasm by spraying water on her vagina as it helps in stimulating the clitoris, labia, and vulva.

Most women masturbate until they reach an orgasm. Although this is slightly tough to achieve for young women, it will get better with age.

When a woman masturbates, she becomes well acquainted with the different pleasure points on her body.

She is better prepared for sex and knows what to expect. Some would think that women will turn pro masturbation and prefer to not have real sex but that is only a myth. A woman will enjoy sex even if she masturbates regularly. In fact, she might experience heightened pleasure during sex if she masturbates regularly.

Some women would wonder if they lose their virginity if they accidently break their hymen while masturbating. But this is a myth. A woman will remain a virgin until she has had sexual intercourse. So breaking of the hymen does not mean loss of virginity. In some cases, virgins will not have a hymen owing to playing aggressive sports or using a tampon and some non-virgins will still have their hymen intact.

Tips:

Here are some masturbation tips that will help you have a better experience when you go solo.

• It is a good idea for you to masturbate when you are alone. The fear of being judged by someone often causes us to not experience heightened pleasure. So, it is important to be completely free and be able to scream out loud when you are pleasured.

• You can improve your mood by watching porn or reading erotic material. These will get you into the right mood and will increase your level of pleasure. If you wish to avoid watching porn, then looking at some sexy pictures or illustrations will do the trick.

• You must also set the right tone in terms of atmosphere. Burn a few aroma candles and play some calming music. You will feel happy and in the mood to masturbate.

• Before stimulating your clitoris, you have to lick your finger or wet it by some means. You can also apply a little oil or lubricant as that will give you a wet feeling and enhance your sexual experience.

• Most women masturbate by lying flat on their back, as that is the most comfortable position. But it is also quite boring. So, you can experiment with your positions and improve your pleasure. You can try the missionary position where you lift your legs and hold them parallel or can also turn around into the doggie position.

• A great way to make it interesting is to alternate your hand and use your non-dominant hand to masturbate. This will introduce an element of surprise and help you experience a different sort of pleasure.

• You can insert a finger or two inside your vagina while stroking your clitoris. This will help you have a great experience. You can use both hands if you wish and insert fingers of one hand and use fingers of the other to stroke your clitoris.

• The G-spot is an area that is located inside your vagina and lies around 2 inches inside. Since it is the most pleasurable part, you have to find and stroke it to pleasure yourself. Don't worry if you don't find it, it generally takes some time for people to find and stroke their G-spot.

• There is nothing wrong in having a quickie with yourself. Some people might not advise it as it takes away from the experience. But if you are not interested in slowly stroking your clitoris and find it easier to jump right into it then you can find your g-spot and start stroking it to have a quick session. What you do to pleasure yourself is entirely up to you and nobody should be telling you what to and what not to do.

• Holding your breath while masturbating helps in availing a better experience. You will feel much better if you exhale while experiencing the orgasm.

• It is possible for you to have an immediate orgasm just as one is dying down. You must immediately start stroking your clitoris once again and that will get you started once again. Many women find the second successive orgasm to be much more pleasurable than the first one.

• Many women don't masturbate at all and that is completely fine. But as was mentioned earlier, doing so increases a woman's level of pleasure. You become more aware of your body and what truly pleasures you.

These tips are sure to help you avail a heightened pleasurable experience.

Precautions to Observe

When it comes to masturbating, you must observe a few precautions. Here they are:

• While inserting anything inside your vagina, you must see if it will pleasure you or hurt you. It is important to pick something smooth. You must avoid making use of sharp objects that might end up causing internal injury.

• You have to make use of lubricant first if you are feeling too dry. If you haven't had enough natural liquid coating the inner walls then you must use some lotion or Vaseline to help the object slide in and out with ease.

• It is sometimes normal to feel weak after masturbating. It generally happens when you have masturbated a lot and your mind is slightly cloudy. The best thing to do is go to sleep, as you will feel much better after a nap.

• Try to wash your hands and your intimate area with soap and water to get rid of germs that might come about when you masturbate.

Following in these tips will help you have a better experience.

Chapter 13
Male Masturbation Importance and Tips

Men also masturbate and it is quite important for them to do so. Men masturbate to remove some sexual liquid that can build up in their bodies. Not removing them will impact their sexual well being.

Most boys masturbate by age 15. Once the secondary sexual characters start to develop, they feel the need to remove the pent up sexual fluids.

Masturbations in males is seen as a healthy habit and something they must take up at least twice a month.

Male masturbation is much different from female masturbation. As you know, many males take it up to remove the built up fluid as opposed to doing it to seek pleasure.

However, men must also take it up to avail a pleasurable experience. Here are techniques that men take to masturbate:

• To start with, men generally place a loose grip around their penis and start stroking it up and down to generate an orgasm.

• Some men will use sex toys that allow them to insert their penis inside an opening and start pushing in and pulling out their penis.

These are the two most common methods that men use to pleasure themselves while going solo. However, there might be more ways that they use, which might be their personal versions of it.

Tips:

• Going hot and cold alternately is said to enhance your sexual pleasure. The trick is to have a bowl of ice-cold water next to you while masturbating. When you are about to reach the end and feel a wave of heat on your hands, you must place the other hand in the tub of water. This will enhance your pleasure and make you experience a heightened sensation. You can also have just an ice cube ready that you can quickly grab while masturbating.

• Many men use the stop and go technique, which gives them a heightened pleasure. While masturbating, they stop in between to wait until the feeling of orgasm subsides. Then again continue and keep repeating this for the next 5 to 6 times in order to make the final orgasm feel really special.

• As is with women, it is a good idea to switch up your hands! You will have the feeling of a stranger (read mysterious woman) pleasing you, which can increase your pleasure quite a bit.

• Many men neglect their scrotum while trying to please their penis. You will experience a new joy if you play with your scrotum while masturbating.

Women are quite lucky in the orgasm department as they can experience many orgasms successively. Men on the other hand will experience just one as soon as they ejaculate. However, men can prolong the occurrence and experience a better pleasure.

Precautions to Observe:

• Using dry hands is best as oily hands might make your penis slip. That can be a bad thing and might also cause unnecessary injury.

• Some men masturbate thinking it is a bad thing. However, it is the exact opposite. You should masturbate in order to maintain a healthy reproductive system.

• You must have a box of tissue ready to catch the secretions and discard it. You must exercise as much cleanliness as possible while masturbating.

• Some men make use of objects such as penis extenders to gain a few extra inches. Before making use of any such objects, it is best to check if they are genuine and will give you the desired results. There are many varieties available and you can buy most online.

• The same extends to pills that are marketed to help you increase the size of your penis. You have to check if they deliver on their promise.

It is important for men to enjoy their session and take some time out for it. There is no point in standing in the bathroom and masturbating.

Veronica Baruwal

Chapter 14
Kamasutra Myths Busted

Here are some myths on the Kama Sutra that we will bust in order to help you understand the topic better.

Myth: Kama sutra only speaks of sex positions

Fact: I'm sure by now you know that this is not true. The Kama sutra is not a book meant to teach you sex positions alone. There is a lot more to it than just that. The book teaches you on all aspects including foreplay, preparing for sex, what to expect, what to do best, etc. There is just so much information that you will not have to turn to any other book to gain information on sex and have a pleasurable sex life by referring to the Kama sutra.

Myth: Kama sutra is outdated

Fact: The Kama Sutra was a book that was way ahead for its time. It is a timeless piece and will never go out of style. The sex positions that are described in it are all unique and meant to give both the man and the woman pleasure. The positions are all exciting and will not transport you to an ancient era. You have to look at it as an interesting set of positions that you can try with your partner and not as just some instructional book that vouches to make your sex life better.

Myth: It will be too much for virgins to take up the positions

Fact: Virgins will get off on the right foot if they start with Kama sutra positions. There is no point in thinking that virgins will have a tough time with it as it contains positions that are slightly advanced. They can begin with the simpler ones that are quite easy for people to get into and have a great experience. Many people regret their first sexual experience owing to it having been weird or unsatisfactory. But with Kama sutra, that issue can be easily tackled and the person will have a great experience.

Myth: Kama sutra is for people looking to improve their sex life

Fact: This is not true at all. Your sex life does not have to be dull or boring for you to take up Kama sutra positions. You can have a regular sex life and spice it up with the sutra positions. The Kama sutra does not really discriminate between those that are highly experienced and those that are not. The positions will satisfy everyone and bring in a lot of pleasure. The book is meant to help you understand the different ways in which you can please your partner and also avail equal pleasure.

Myth: It will take only a little while to get through the position

Fact: This is not true at all. The Kama sutra is a big book and will take you some time to go through it and understand everything. You can make it a point to read it with your partner in bed, which will get you started. It is not important for you to be in a sexual position each time as you can go through the rest of the book and have a pleasurable time. On the other hand, as you know, there are around 69 different positions that are described and trying all will take you some time and keep you busy for quite some time. And these positions are not all meant to help you have intercourse alone. There are many positions that teach you oral sex and other such positions.

Myth: You have to be Hindu to practice Kama sutra

Fact: This is a very big myth that needs to be busted. Kama sutra has no religious significance whatsoever. Although it was written in India and describes the tales of Lord Kama, it is not important for you to be a Hindu. You can belong to any religion and take up the different sex positions mentioned in the book and pleasure your partner.

Myth: You will still need enhancements and enlargers

Fact: This is not true. Although consuming supplements is a personal choice, you will not need it if you are following the Kama sutra positions. As you know, these positions give you a lot of confidence and also states that size does not really matter. In fact, it promotes small sized penises and states that it is the positions and angles that matter. So, you need not worry about the size of your penis when you are getting into Kama sutra positions.

Myth: The Kama sutra is only for straight people

Fact: This is not true. Although homosexuals might not have been present at the time, that does not have to stop people from using the positions on others of the same sex in today's day and age. Some of the positions can easily be followed by homosexuals as well. In fact, all can be followed by making use of the right angles and a few props. In some of the sculptures that are present in certain temples in India, there are many depictions of two or more women pleasing each other and also certain depictions of group sex.

Myth: Sex will get boring with the same partner

Fact: It is common for people to think that once they have tried out all the different positions with their partner, it will get boring once again. But this is only a myth. Nobody can get bored of repeating a sex position with the same partner. It goes to a different degree each time and will not be monotonous.

Myth: Once I start with Kama sutra, I won't be able to have regular sex

Fact: This is just a myth. A person will not get addicted to Kama sutra and even if he or she does, there is nothing wrong with it. There are some regular positions that are mentioned in the book as well and you don't really have to forget about it entirely. You will of course not feel like getting into some of the complicated positions all the time and reserve it for special occasions alone.

These form some of the myths that surround the Kama sutra and I hope you've had your doubts cleared away effectively.

Chapter 15
Other Arts Related to Kamasutra

It is obvious that the Kama sutra is a wide topic and there are many fields that it influences. For all those interested in having a little more from your experience than just giving and seeking pleasure, here are some parallel arts that you can pursue in order to enhance your experience.

In reality, there are around 64 different art forms that are related to the Kamasutra, according to Vatsyayana, the writer of Kama sutra.

However, we will look at a few of the most prominent ones in this chapter.

Singing

It is possible for you to impress your partner through singing. India is known to have produced some of the most prolific singers and they have sung some awe-inspiring songs. There is a lot of emphasis on singing songs while making love because it helps in bringing your partner closer to you. The two of you will connect on a deeper level and will be lost in each other's sweet voices. There is no particular emphasis on the type of song that needs to be sung and anything that pleases you and is in your comfort zone can be sung.

Dancing

Dance and Kamasutra have a very deep connection. As you can see from most of the positions, they are mostly inspired by dance positions. Dancers have the tendency of contorting their bodies into the different positions and pleasing their partner. So, by taking up dancing, you will be able to get into the positions easily and won't have to put too much effort towards it. You can take up jazz or tango with your partner. The two of you will be able to spend more time with each other and also get into each other's comfort zones.

Playing an Instrument

Doesn't matter if you are not a good singer or possess a great voice. You can play an instrument and impress her just as well. It can be an instrument of your choice but try picking one that produces a melodious sound. Something like a ukulele or a flute will help you set the right tone. But a guitar will also work well as long as you play romantic tunes. You can record a tune and play it while trying out the positions with your partner.

Poetry

Poetry also has a deep connection with Kama sutra. It is a great way for a man to impress his lady by reading out a poem. In fact, with a poem you can win over a girl's heart and make her fall in love with you. But you must ensure that the poem is original and you have put in an effort to make it sound impressive. You can go through some of the most romantic poems of all time and draw your inspiration from it. Incorporating small elements that you know will impress her will go a long way in you winning her heart.

Drawing

The Kama sutra is a book that is full of illustrations. These illustrations are all meant to help you understand the different positions better. As you know, a picture speaks a thousand words. So, to impress your ladylove, you can make interesting pictures for her. These pictures can depict your love for your lady and illustrate to her how deeply you love her. You can then get the pictures framed and give it to her to use as décor. You can also take a picture of it and send her a soft copy to have on her cell phone. Drawing something sensual will surely get her into the right mood.

Tattooing

You can make use of a tattoo to impress her as well. If you have a creation that she really loves, then consider getting it on a part of your body, which only she can see. That will make it extra special for the two of you. The tattoo need not be too elaborate and can be a toned down version of the picture that you have in mind. If you don't want anything of a permanent nature, then you can get a henna tattoo. These are temporary tattoos but will help you have a detailed one nonetheless.

Types of Love

According to the Kama sutra, there are 4 types of love that exist in this world and they are as follows:

Love acquired through habit

The first type of love is that which is acquired as a result of continued practice. The person might not inherently love the practice but will take a liking to it as a result of performing it every now and then. For example, the love for smoking or drinking will come about as a consequence of taking it up regularly. Similarly, the love for intercourse will also come about for similar reasons.

Love as a result of imagination

The next type of love is said to come through as a result of vivid imagination. Some people have a great sense of imagination and are capable of dreaming lucidly. They imagine things and then fall in love with what they see in it. It is important for people to have a single, straight stream of thought that they can pursue. That will help them imagine vividly and develop a love for what they imagine.

Some people imagine an ideal girl or woman and fall in love with her.

Love as a result of belief

Love as a result of belief is known as one where the person nurtures certain beliefs that he or she thinks to be true of the other person. For example, a person thinks that his new partner is someone he knows for a long time and will find it easy to connect deeply with them. The belief may or may not be based on a proven fact. It might be a result of a thought that the person generates in his mind and assumes it to be the absolute truth.

Love resulting from external perception

Some might call this lust but it is also arguably a feeling of love that arises when a person likes or loves another for what they look like or how they are perceived. External appearance plays a big role in people falling in love and it is only possible for two people to love each other deeply if they like each other's looks. It is quite rare to find someone who does not judge another for his or her appearance and falls in love nonchalantly.

These form the 4 types of love that the Kamasutra describes in detail.

Veronica Baruwal

Chapter 16
Aphrodisiacs and Supplements to Try Out

It is obvious that your capacity to have sex can deplete over a period of time. This can show on both your mental and physical capacity. You will therefore need to consume supplements and eat aphrodisiacs to improve your mood.

Aphrodisiacs refer to those foods that increase your capacity to have sex. They help you get into the right mood.

Here is what you can consume to improve your mood.

Aphrodisiacs for Women

Cacao

Have you ever bitten into a chocolate and wanted to jump into bed with your partner? That is mainly because of its coco contents. Cacao or coco is a great aphrodisiac for women. Coco contains phenyl ethylamine, which is a chemical that increases women's libido. It also helps during sex by releasing dopamine, which is needed to have a great experience in bed. So, the next time you wish to have a great session, just bite into that chocolate!

Fenugreek

Fenugreek is a plant that produces bitter tasting leaves and small brown seeds. Both of these are quite effective in helping you increase your libido. You can crush the leaves slightly and add them to soups and salads or roast the seeds lightly and crush it to add to your curries. You can also gulp down some warm water with the roasted seeds added to it. It also helps in increasing breast milk, which assists in lactation.

Shatavari

Shatavari is a root that is used to improve women's sexuality. It is a root that has been used for a very long time to aid in strengthening the reproductive system. A strong system will help a woman remain interested in sex for a long time. In fact, it is alternately known as "she who has 1000 husbands" which signifies how much it aids in keeping her strong and ready. Shatavari is generally available in powder form and it is dissolved in a glass of water before consuming.

Dates

Dates are a great aphrodisiac for women. They can warm you on the inside and contain a lot of nutrients and fiber. These will make you fit and healthy. You can develop strength and vigor to have sex on a regular basis. Dates can be had in any form. Being sweet, they make for great additions to sweet dishes and milkshakes. You can also buy the dry variety and crush them to add to your drinks.

Coriander seeds

Coriander seeds help in warming up the internal organs and prepare the woman for sex. The seeds can be lightly toasted and added to boiling water before consuming them. Some women also prepare a small pouch with boiled leaves and seeds and insert it into their vagina. That helps them warm up and prepare for a session.

Chilies

Hot chilies can also get women's libido going. Chilies provide the right amount of heat. You can chop a few and add them to your curries or soups. Consuming it regularly will help you increase your libido.

These are some of the foods that women can consume to increase their libido. But don't do all at once. Try each of them separately and then stick with the one that works best for you.

Aphrodisiacs for Men

Just like women, men will also need some help. In fact, they might need it more than women as many men start to tire out and lose interest in sex as they age. Here are some aphrodisiacs for men to try.

Ashwagandha

Ashwagandha is a root that is widely grown in Asia. It is widely consumed in Asian countries by men wanting to increase their libido and sexual activity. You can buy some ready tablets or find the root itself that you can crush and add to some water before consuming. However, you might have to ask a physician about it first before consuming it.

Maca root

Maca root is another natural root that you can use to increase your libido. It is said to establish hormonal balance, which is quite necessary to have a proper libido. It is available online and the pack will contain the right dosage that you have to consume. Here too, you must ask a physician first before consuming it.

Mussels

Mussels are some of the most sought after aphrodisiacs for men. They contain a chemical that is said to instantly boost a man's sexual energy. Mussels are also full of nutrition that will increase a person's level of energy. Consuming mussels on a regular basis is a must for men who are finding it tough to have the mood for sex. You can simply roast some in garlic oil and consume.

Almonds

Almonds contain several nutrients that are great for your body. Right from vitamin B2 to vitamin E, your body will avail many nutrients. Asians and Arabians have consumed almonds for several centuries to improve their libido and sexual prowess. Almonds are very easy to incorporate in your diet and you can chew on some on a daily basis.

Honey

Honey is also a great aphrodisiac that you can try. It cools the body down, which is needed for men to produce enough semen. Honey can be incorporated in many ways. You can add a tablespoon of it to your morning tea or can also add it to milk and consume. Honey can also be drizzled on fruit salads or regular salads. You have to buy natural honey though, which is sourced from natural bee farms. You must avoid the ones that have chemicals added in.

Artichoke

Artichokes can be a great addition to your diet. You can cut up a few and add to your curries or roast them. Fresh artichokes can also be steamed and added to your curries. You can also season it with salt and pepper and consume.

Avocados

Avocados are also great for your libido. You can cut up and add some to your salads. You can also cut some and add to smoothies or milkshakes.

Veronica Baruwal

Key Highlights

First and foremost, you must understand what the Kama sutra is all about. In this day and age, where there are so many technological advancements that help people have a near real sexual experience without having to have a partner; people have truly forgotten to connect with their real partners. This can be a big problem as it defeats the logics of science and reproduction. Man can try but will not be able to avail true pleasure or be able to reproduce with a machine. Therefore, the need of the hour is to introduce people to something that will get them to appreciate real sex with a partner and stop being satisfied with sex toys.

The Kama sutra is the oldest book known to man that was based on love, relationships, and sex. The book gives an insight into what love, relationships, and sex should be carried out as and why it is important for people to appreciate these simple aspects of life. The book was written by an Indian saint known as Vatsyayana and he is said to have written it between 200 and 400 BC.

The book has vivid illustrations of sexual positions that people can carry out. These positions are all meant to help you derive increased pleasure and beat the monotony. These positions have also been carved on the pillars of Hindu temples in India and are said to be quite descriptive.

The Kama sutra lays down a few ideologies that are meant to help people improve their sexual experiences. First, it speaks about how women should be prepared for sex and enjoy it just as much as men. Back in the day, most women were forced to get married and have sex. They would mostly not be prepared for it and not enjoy it as much. But the Kama sutra laid emphasis on the importance of women's pleasure. The next ideology lays emphasis on the size of the penis and how smaller ones are most ideal for women to derive pleasure. It lays a lot of emphasis on consensual sex and why it should always be a two-sided affair.

As per the Kama sutra, it is extremely important for people to lead a healthy lifestyle if they wish to have a great experience in bed. A good diet will go a long way in having a great sex life.

It is extremely important for people to try out new sex positions and not stick to the same old ones. Some people tend to get quite comfortable with certain positions and don't really experiment. The book showcases 69 different positions that people can adopt and spice up their sex life.

Sex is considered a leisurely activity and not something that is hurried. In fact, it takes place in many stages and not in one go. People have to remain patient and enjoy the entire journey. There are 5 main steps of great sex and it starts with courtship. The two people wanting to have sex should love each other and have a desire to unite sexually. The man must put in efforts to please the girl. Second comes seduction. Here, the man should make the girl comfortable in love and wanting to have a sexual experience. Consent is extremely important for sex. Next comes foreplay. Foreplay is to prepare the body for the experience that is to come. The next step is to have sex by getting into the different positions that are elaborated in the book. Finally, it is extremely important for the man to take care of the girl after the session has ended. He must speak to her and take care of her.

The Kama sutra lays a lot of emphasis on the man taking the lead and pleasing his partner. He even removes the clothes of his partner in a gentle manner and gets her into the right mood. There is also emphasis on some rough foreplay where it is allowed to bite or scratch your partner. When people are having intercourse, if the woman bites the man then he will penetrate her deeper, which will cause her to clench and produce better pleasure.

We looked at many sex positions from the Kama sutra and also read their description in detail. You can go through them again if you wish to perfect it for your partner. You can also have the book open and ready while having sex in order to look at it and perform the poses with ease.

We also looked at tantric sex positions that you can try out. As you now know, tantric sex is a technique that you use to remain connected with your partner for a long time and keep pleasuring them. You must remember that women can go on well past reaching an orgasm and it is important for her to reach there first. That will help you have a prolonged experience and you can delay your orgasm as long as you like.

The Kama sutra clearly mentions the type of women who are ideal candidates to have sex with and those that are not suitable. This list was mostly meant to help men of the time pick women to be their consort.

The Kama sutra lays emphasis on masturbation. Masturbation is the art of pleasing oneself and the person can derive a lot of pleasure by engaging in it. Women, especially, must engage in masturbation as it aids in knowing which points help them avail most pleasure. They will be able to guide their partners and the two of them can experience heightened pleasure.

We busted several myths on the topic to help you understand it better. These myths prevent some people from enjoying themselves fully and you must move past them to have a great experience with your partner.

There are some parallel arts that you can study along with the Kama sutra and they will help you connect with it in a better way. They are meant to enhance your experience and increase your love for pleasure.

Conclusion

Over the course of reading this book, you may have begun to realize that Kama Sutra is ancient knowledge, but it also begins to seem like common sense after you have read about it. Only about one-fifth of the original Kama Sutra was actually concerned with sexual positions, yet this is what most people tend to concentrate on. The rest of it is more about the relationships between men and women, useful insights on the game of love, and living a good and fulfilling life. It's a sort of third century relationship advice compendium, even though it's actually addressed to a man.

Ancient texts like the Kama Sutra were written in a time where humans were a lot more in tune with their inner selves. They also saw sex as something natural, holy, and sacred, and part of a loving relationship. Sex itself was not considered sinful, which is why there were so many extenuating circumstances that allowed men to more or less have sex with whomever they wanted, subject to certain conditions. However, having bad sex was considered unpardonable, which is why the advice regarding sex is so detailed, to the point where modern readers think it is boring rather than titillating, and they would rather just look at the pictures!

You should now be well on the path to living a fuller life by applying the principles of Kama Sutra, if you have taken on board the advice and suggestions in this book, and used the background information to fully understand the Kama Sutra mindset.

Hopefully you will soon be able to enjoy putting the things you have learned in this book into practice. Just remember, Kama Sutra is not a onetime sex trick that you can use whenever you want to and then discard, it is a way of life! Use the information provided in this book as a way to live your life, and you should be more relaxed and sexually fulfilled than ever before.

Manufactured by Amazon.ca
Bolton, ON

33819724R00098